The Truths of Others

An Essay on
Nativistic Intellectuals in Mexico

Alicja Iwańska

*To Professor Lynch
with best wishes

Alicja Iwańska*

SCHENKMAN PUBLISHING COMPANY, INC.
Cambridge, Massachusetts 02138

Copyright © 1977

Schenkman Publishing Company, Inc.
3 Mt. Auburn Place
Cambridge, Massachusetts 02138

Library of Congress Cataloging in Publication Data

Iwanska, Alicja.
    The truths of others.

    1. Indians of Mexico—Government relations.
2. Social movements—Mexico. 3. Indians of Mexi-
co—Race   identity. 4. Nativistic   movements—
Mexico.
I. Title.
F1219.3.G6I92   301.24'2'0972   76-40139
ISBN 0-87073-558-6 cloth
ISBN 0-87073-559-4 paper

Printed in the United States of America

Contents

Acknowledgments

Gratitude and respect for those whom I interviewed and consulted in order to write this book are amply documented on its pages.

To all others who gave me advice (which I did not always follow), encouragement and help and to Mrs. Pat Wiles who typed the manuscript—many thanks.

The first drafts of this book were read carefully and honestly evaluated by two colleagues from my university, Prof. Paul Wheeler from the Sociology Department and Prof. Robert Carmack from the Department of Anthropology. Professor Sol Tax from the University of Chicago (who years ago helped me to get involved in my Mexican research) gave his anthropological "blessings" to the last version of my manuscript, while my friend, Maria Zych, read it carefully from the perspective of our common Polish past and common hopes for the future. Sharman Braff from Schenkman Publishing Co. made very intelligent and helpful editorial suggestions.

The research on which this book is based was subsidized by a grant from the Research Foundation of the State University of New York.

All royalties from the sale of this book go to the Mazahua Child Scholarship Fund which I created in connection with my research in the Mazahua area. This fund is administered by Instituto Indigenista Interamericano in Mexico.

A. I.

INTRODUCTION

1. About This Book

This is a book about two social movements organized by Mexican natives with higher education during the late 1940s. Both movements operate from their seats in Mexico City, both have existed for almost thirty years.

It is generally assumed that in a mestizo country like Mexico, where practically everybody is partially of indigenous origin and no racial ideology exists, every native with higher education would become acculturated to European-like Mexican ways, and consider himself Mexican.

But this is not always the case. The numerous social movements that emerged after the Second World War as a consequence of large-scale decolonization in Africa and Asia influenced the rise of similar movements among indigenous, racial and ethnic minorities all over the world. Even the most acculturated natives in Mexico, as elsewhere in the decolonized world, started questioning the places assigned to them by the dominant groups within their societies, and began searching for ways to assert themselves within those societies and in the larger world.

All Mexican natives are invited to full Mexican citizenship (which means the European, predominantly Spanish, and recently strongly U. S.-influenced, life style). It is assumed that all educated natives would accept these ideological invitations. If they do not, it is considered an uncomfortable anomaly, something which the majority of Mexicans would prefer not to perceive. The truths of others are not easily recognized.

1

The participants in the two social movements presented in this book did not accept the nation's ideological invitation to become Mexicans, or, having been already Mexicans for some time, through their parents or their own decisions, they rejected Mexican identification. Though assumed to be Mexicans because of their higher education, acculturation and professional status, they chose instead to identify with their native groups, and work on behalf of their people.

The members of the first movement, whom I named "Realists" (they described themselves frequently as "realists" or "pragmatists" in conversations with me), challenge mainly the Government's strategies of integration of the Indian masses into Mexican society. This integration should be done, according to them, under the leadership of educated natives like themselves, born and raised in Indian villages and maintaining unbroken contacts with their people.

The members of the second movement, whom I named "Utopians," (because of their ambitious ideology of a total restructuring of Mexican society) are fully acculturated urban people, generally. They refer to themselves as "Nahuas," "Mexicans" (in the sense of aboriginal *Mexicas*), "Aztecs" and "Anauakians." Their program is ambitious indeed, since they have been promoting nothing less than a peaceful transformation of Mexico into a modernized Confederation of Anauak, or Aztec Empire, as it is usually known.

Though I doubt very much whether we could study any country without taking into account its history, the historical dimension is of particular importance for understanding contemporary Mexico. Due to a variety of factors in this dynamic modern republic we find not only colonial structural units (both administrative and religious) but even precolonial social structures, such as ancient clans, *calpullis* for instance, or undefeated groups of nomadic northern Mexican natives.

The historical perspective which the reader should keep in mind while reading this book starts with the rise of Nahuatl-speaking Aztecs, and their establishment of an enormous, highly civilized state which several centuries later, in 1521, was invaded and defeated by Spaniards. Whether we call it "Aztec Empire" or "Confederation of Anauak" this state was definitely what Florian Znaniecki would call a "religious culture society:"[1] its literary culture, like Hindu, Islamic or Judaic cultures, was based on sacred (religious) rather than on secular books. Its leaders and prophets were religiously trained men, and all its institutions had a combined secular-religious character. Aztec-dominated Mexico was a truly theocratic totalitarian state.

Though it was a multinational and multitribal type of society in which over 200 languages were spoken[2] and where class differences were prominent, we may assume that in this society some basic congruence did exist between the world view of the heterogeneous multilingual masses and the cosmology of their governing elites. There was, probably, some basic agreement on such sociologically significant concepts as value of land, authority, family and religion. In spite of periodic political turmoils the moral order of the people of precolonial Mexico remained, probably, unbroken.

In Colonial Mexico (1521-1810) in spite of important structural similarities in the political system of the invaders (Aztec totalitarian theocracy was replaced by Spanish totalitarian theocracy), the moral order of the native masses was from the very start of the invasion badly shaken and broken. This was done probably, not so much through the imposition of different religious and political systems, but rather through the completely different attitudes of the Spaniards toward native elites and through their completely foreign patterns of domination and subordination. The Spaniards' ways of imposing, demanding, restraining, patronizing and rewarding were diametrically opposed to those of the Aztecs. This incongruence between the native world view and colonial ideology, though very acute, and sometimes even harmful to their own interests, was very likely unperceived by the colonial elites.

Post-Colonial Mexico (1810 until the present) was designed as a "national culture society": nontotalitarian, open, democratic, secular. The governing elites, first creoles, later mestizos, have been from the very beginning acutely aware of the painful and dangerous incongruence between the world view of the Indian masses and their own national ideology. Various attempts have been made by the government and numerous political and intellectual groups to build up a "Mexican nationality"[3] in this culturally heterogeneous and socially disharmonious state.[4]

When we compare the power elites of today's post-colonial societies we shall notice that they vary considerably in regard to their "racial"[5] and cultural components. Power elites of the United States, Canada, Chile, Argentina and Uruguay, for instance, have been both "racially" and culturally European, while the power elites of Mexico, Guatemala, Peru, and Bolivia have been "racially" mestizo and culturally European. On the other hand, India, Ghana and many other new Asian and African nations have had truly native, though often culturally European, power elites. Within our increasingly shrinking modern world affected by rapid transportation and the spread of mass media, it is hard to imagine the emergence of both "racially" and culturally native power elites, whatever the great dreams of nativistic leaders may be.

Both social movements presented in this book are deeply committed to the creation of native power elites in Mexico. They promote however their own distinct and sometimes contradictory ways of implementing this dream.

If we say that "a social movement occurs when a fairly large number of people band together in order to alter or supplement some portion of the existing culture or social order"[6] then some types of social movements do, probably, exist in all societies, "primitive" and "civilized." They take, however, a different form and often are called by different names in societies culturally and structurally different. In totalitarian societies social movements cannot usually operate openly, unless sponsored by the government. They function, usually, more or less underground, and are branded as deviations, crimes, heresies. In open, democratic societies social movements are generally allowed and even encouraged to function openly. Sometimes even those which promote the creation of a state within the state (if defined as harmless and marginal) are permitted to reinforce the democratic ideology.

In modern, bureaucratized, relatively stable societies which have democratic or, like Mexico, semidemocratic political structures, the very existence of social movements means an important assertion of individual freedom and creativity. Those movements, whether religious, cultural and even ecological or political in a stricter sense, always represent some attempt to say or do something which has not been achieved by the official national institutions. Whatever the deficiencies of a given democracy (and there are no perfect democracies in existence), the possibility of the emergence of an accepted or tolerated social movement proves that a given country does not have a totalitarian character. Only in such countries can sociologists study social movements *in vivo*. I could not study social movements *in vivo* in the Soviet Union nor in contemporary Brazil or Chile!

The two social movements presented in this book and the identity dilemmas of their members, though described within the context of Mexico in 1973, should be seen within the context of the whole decolonized contemporary world and the turmoils and aspirations of its people. The conflict between the ideal of social justice to which the Mexican Indian "Realists" are committed, and the ideal of cultural self-realization, through the revival of cultural continuity, prominent in the thought and action of Nahua "Utopians," is of particular importance in today's decolonized world.[7]

Though in many technologically simple societies equality has been truly practiced, old civilizations, such as those of the Incas and the Aztecs, were never concerned with social justice in the sense of equal opportunity and equal treatment for all with strong emphasis on economic and educational variables. Far more, however, than many equality-proclaiming nations, they were concerned with the cultural rights of the peoples living within the boundaries of their culturally heterogeneous states. Their deities, customs and languages were generally respected, and their dignity was not so badly damaged as that of many cultural minorities of today.

The Mexican Indian "Realists," committed to social justice for Indian masses, decided to support (on their own terms however) the national Mexican policy of integration of the natives into the national culture. Though they deplore the loss of native cultures, they assume this to be an inevitable development. The sooner this integration occurs, they believe, the less the deprivation and suffering of the Indian masses.

The "Utopians" have made an opposite choice. They do not assume immediate responsibility for economic and social deprivations suffered by the Mexican natives but they do concern themselves with their future cultural well-being, without which—they argue—no social well-being, no overcoming of underdevelopment, corruption and economic dependency can ever be achieved in Mexico.

If a tragic situation consists of an inevitable choice between two equally cherished values, (this definition is based on Max Scheler's reflections on tragedy) then both "Realists" and "Utopians" have been forced, indeed, into such a tragic choice between the ideal of social justice on the one hand and that of cultural self-realization on the other—choices spared to other more lucky humans.

2. Interviews and Other Contacts

I arrived in Mexico City in the spring of 1973 to study Mexican natives with higher education. I had assumed that I would have a hard time locating them, and I certainly did not expect to find more than a handful of such individuals. But during the very first week a helpful librarian[8] from the *Instituto Indigenista Interamericano*[9] gave me a pile of thin bi-weeklies called *Cuadernos del AMPII (Asociación Mexicana de los Profesionales e Intelectuales Indígenas*, Association of Mexican Indian Professionals and Intellectuals). Through this magazine I established quite easily my first contacts with those educated native Mexicans whom I later named "Realists." They had a great respect and friendship for the founder and leader of their association[10], and that is why, I am sure, they agreed so readily to be interviewed by me.

I was given a quaint little cubical in the building of the *Instituto Indigenista Interamericano*, but only two of the thirteen members of AMPII whom I interviewed came to this little office. Most of them preferred to be interviewed in their own offices, and I used to meet them very early in the morning before they started their work or very late in the afternoon after their work was finished. This way we were generally alone and undisturbed by telephone calls.

Since I was well recommended by their movement's leader, had had the experience of many years of work among Mexican natives, and could give them a copy of my book on the Mazahuas (recently translated into Spanish),[11] the rapport was generally very good. I had to explain, of course, the purpose of my study and to tell them quite a bit about myself in the beginning of every interview. Interviewing persons with higher education is usually both educative and embarrassing. We learn much from our interviewees but we get embarrassed about our own ignorance as well. My own cultural marginality—the fact that I have been for many years a political exile from Poland, was educated in Poland, Belgium and the United States, and had conducted research in Mexico—helped additionally, I believe, in establishing rapport.

On a few occasions my first contacts resulted in interesting confrontations. Once I was literally interviewed by one of these men, who asked me many difficult questions, probing deeply into my own identity. He asked how I combined my being a Polish exile and having American citizenship, why I left Poland and came to live in the United States, and why I studied Mexican natives, so far away from my place of residence (Albany, New York), while living within the boundaries of the Northamerican Iroquois Federation.

I was pleased with such confrontations, so customary among Polish intelligentsia and considered such "bad taste" in the United States. They reinforced, somehow, my own identity and helped to establish an even better rapport with my interviewees as well.

Making contact with the members of the second social movement, the "Utopians," was not so prompt and easy. I heard about them from the "Realists" who referred to them as "Aztec intellectuals," "Nahua intellectuals," or as "intellectuals from the Academy of Nahuatl"; they called them "aristocrats," "racists," "phony," "mysterious," "unrealistic politicians," "mystics," "idealists," "opportunists." They were spoken of as being a "Nahua underground government" or as being "just one of the many political platforms in Mexico." The "Realists" spoke about them with anger, resentment, curiosity, admiration, embarrassment. But no one from among the "Realists" had easy access to this group.

Finally, seeing my distress, one of my interviewees, the best informed and most respectful toward "those Nahuas," decided to give me a name and office address of one of this movement's prominent leaders, a well-known Mexican professional, "ingeniero X," whom he did not, however, know personally. He told me to go to his office and tell him that I was recommended by an old acquaintance of the movement's deceased leader licenciado Rodolfo Nieva. This was not the best introduction, but since I did not have any other, I decided to try my luck.

It is not easy to study a semi-secret political sect. It is more difficult to study it in a foreign society. It is even harder to get access to such a sect with an introduction as fragile as the one I had. But following the custom I had established with the first group, I gave "ingen_ero X" (I have disguised the identities of all persons I refer to in this book) a copy of my book, my visiting card and a copy of my work-plan. After about ten days he called to tell me that the members of the movement did not have anything against my study and would make available to me all written materials, but that they did not wish to be interviewed. He assured me, however, that I could call him whenever I needed any help with my research. I spent more than a month in the library going carefully through over fifteen years of the movement's monthly magazine, *Izkalotl,* and called ingeniero X whenever I had any doubts about something I read. We became well acquainted through those telephone conversations, and I gained enough of his confidence to be invited to several lectures and one Aztec ceremony at the very end of my stay in Mexico. I was also invited to the celebration of the coming of the Aztec New Year on the eve of December 22, and returned to Mexico for my winter vacation in order to participate in this ceremony. This invitation led to another invitation to a ceremony held out of town. Some data from this unexpected participant observation are included in various chapters of this book.

Though I met many members of this movement personally on the occasion of those lectures and ceremonies I did not make any attempt either to take photographs of the ceremonies or to conduct interviews. Those were gestures of friendship—I assumed—rather than research situations.

I have to mention, however, an incident that occurred during the third Aztec ceremony of Assignment of Names (*Asignacion de Nombres*), to which I was invited on the first day of the Aztec New Year, *Conejo 1* (Year of Rabbit 1), Dec. 22, together with a Polish friend, who came to join me from England. All through this ceremony, which took place on a small isolated farm a couple of hours from Mexico City and was attended by many of the Movement's members and many Nahua natives from the area, we deliberately avoided mixing with the participants. We had both agreed that the first invitation to closer encounter should not come from us.

After several hours, when the ceremony and the outdoor feast were over, a middle-aged man, in fact the movement's leader as I found out soon afterwards, approached us with a few other men and women and, giving us a piece of paper and pencil, asked us to write as clearly as possible our names so he could introduce us to the group, as was customary during such gatherings. We talked with him for a few minutes and then we all assembled in a circle to begin a long series of speeches, commentaries to speeches and announcements.

At the conclusion the leader introduced us as the guests of the movement, saying that the movement had always been inspired by the history of our country, Poland, which has been heroically fighting two powerful, aggressive enemies, Germans and Russians, for centuries. He was very well-informed, indeed, not only about the Nazi occupation of Poland but about the murder of thousands of Polish officers by Soviet Russians in the forest of Katyń,[12] as well.

We were both amazed and moved. My friend, who has been living in England since World War Two, whispered to me that it was incredible, indeed, that she had to come to those highlands of Nahuatl-speaking natives to learn that there are some people who do know about Katyń. . . . "I wish," she said, "that my English friends, who are after all Europeans, were as well informed about our national tragedies. . . . "

BACKGROUND

1. Ideological Confusions

More energetically than many other postcolonial countries of our era, Mexico has been struggling to form its national culture, national solidarity, and national identification. Like other developing nations it seeks to assert its economic independence within the world of more and more interwoven economic interests, technologies, and the more and more influential U. S. mass media.[1]

In order to understand the tremendous difficulties involved in the creation of national culture in Mexico, we have to remember that, in spite of some unifying influences of the Aztec political system, this area remained strongly heterogeneous, composed of hundreds of culturally distinct groups, and that it was invaded by a group of Spaniards coming from a variety of social strata and subcultures. Sixteenth century Spain, despite its national language, could hardly be called a well-formed nationality. A transnational ideology of Catholicism and common interests in gaining gold, glory and a comfortable life were the major unifying forces of this small group of invaders, who after the fall of Tenochtitlan on August 13, 1521, controlled the territory of today's Mexico.

The National ideology of Mexican Independence (1810), though strongly anti-Spanish in its sentiments and full of invocations to the glorified "Aztec forefathers," remained, nevertheless, deeply rooted in Catholicism. The marianist cult of the "Indian" Virgen de Guadalupe was an essential element of this first Mexican national ideology. This myth of a Mexican nation, strongly Catholic, and at the same time

9

carrying on the traditions of ancient Aztecs,[2] (mainly creole Catholic clergy) though helpful as an ideological weapon in the war against peninsular Spaniards, was never consistently elaborated nor did it ever gain popular acceptance. It "nationalized," so to say, the basically transnational ideology of Catholicism but it never managed to "nationalize" the "Aztec forefathers."

In fact, until the Revolution of 1910, Catholicism remained the only consistent ideology which helped the rulers (first the colonial ones, then the leaders of the first century of independent Mexico) to govern this culturally and socially disunified territory. All attempts at replacing this popular Catholicism, either with liberalism or with egalitarianism, had failed in Mexico. No solid, consistent and comprehensible ideology of social justice had so far been developed in this country.[3] Often misunderstood by their promoters, those ideals remained largely incomprehensible to the Mexican masses. We may argue that in spite of the persecution of the Catholic Church by the Mexican Revolution, Catholic folklore[4] is still today a powerful unifying force in Mexico.

Had there been an attempt by Mexican governments to reform rather than reject Catholicism (to further restrict the power of priests and free Catholic dogmas from bureaucratic additions) maybe the national unity of Mexico would have become much stronger than it is today. But at that time there were no models of progressive Catholicism within their reach, and Mexican intellectuals were too busy with the postrevolutionary reconstruction of their country, and too isolated to search actively for such models.

Mexican postrevolutionary national ideology was supposed to be as "native" as possible and it was to be quickly available. The vague ideology of a mestizo "cosmic race," formulated by José Vasconcelos in 1920,[5] tried to serve for some time the goal of national unification. It glorified (within the context of Latin America) the new dynamic Mexican nation, the nation "born of two bloods and two cultures," Indian and Spanish, and proclaimed the Latin American population to be "more vigorous, more dynamic, more intelligent, more sensitive" than other populations, especially their northern Anglo Saxon neighbors. This "cosmic race" of Latin America was, eventually, to humanize the rest of the world, and to provide it with leadership.

Unlike its neighbor, the United States, in which strong racial thinking has created barriers between "whites" and "colored populations" of Blacks, Chicanos, Puerto Ricans and Orientals, Mexico has been, throughout its national existence, a predominantly mestizo country. Its population, through rape, mating and marriage, started mixing genetically during the first decades of Spanish occupation. Though some generalized racial prejudice toward darker people (without awareness, however, of the differences between negroid and mongoloid stock) still exists in today's Mexico, "racial thinking" did not color either the ideology or the laws of the Mexican Republic.[6] Since the Revolution of 1910, Mexican national ideology has been strongly pro-native, emphasizing the "Indian input" into the "Spanish-Indian" culture of the country far more than the Spanish input.

In spite of this insistence, which has made some foreign visitors conclude that Mexico was an "Indian country," culturally Mexico has been far more European than Indian. The non-acculturated native population has been left economically, politically and educationally behind, neglected, or, at best, misunderstood, by Mexican national ideologists. It became reduced to a large, usually undifferentiated and uncomfortable "minority," a painful "social problem." Those natives whose clusters have culturally survived became the nation's "chief national problem"—as we read often in Mexican press—the "problem" whose "solution" has been seen in the cultural disappearance of natives from the Mexican scene.

There are no "ethnic groups" in contemporary Mexico, if by "ethnic group" we understand a group of foreign origin, incorporated and basically acculturated into the national society but maintaining some of the native cultural characteristics. But there are many foreign "colonies" in Mexico which enjoy high prestige, French, American, Spanish, just to mention a few. Mexican natives are neither "ethnic groups" nor even "foreigners" in their own country. In fact, they do not today fit into any social category. Ideologically glorified, always talked about and bringing much tourist money to Mexico, they have been painfully pushed aside as they carry on their more and more impoverished culture on the margins of the national society.[7]

2. Invitation to Heroism

President Lázaro Cárdenas (1934-1940) was a great implementor of the Mexican Revolution rather than its ideologist. The vague social philosophy of a glorified "mestizo race" was still prevalent during his presidency. Without questioning this philosophy, and being deeply concerned with the implementation of revolutionary ideals of social justice, Cárdenas announced that education in Mexico was going to be "socialistic," that is, would "combat fanaticism and prejudices and . . . help young people to form rational and exact concepts of both the universe and social life."[8] But the term "socialism," used without qualification during the decade of major crimes committed in Soviet Russia,[9] and within a firmly capitalistic society, served only to antagonize some conservative strata, without changing the philosophy of education in any fundamental way.[10] Without such philosophical changes he managed nevertheless to deeply affect the social structure of Mexico and especially that of Mexican natives who still speak of him with great affection and respect.

In the name of implementation of the laws formulated during the Mexican Revolution, much land was confiscated from the great landowners and distributed to people of rural origin (most of them natives) throughout Mexico. Education was made obligatory for all (fines were imposed upon those parents who would not send their children to school) and expense-free Indian boarding schools, many with bilingual teachers, were opened throughout the country.

This was a great moment for Mexican natives. For the first time since the Spanish invasion, they were offered at least one avenue to enter en masse the national society. Through education in those schools and subsequent returning to their respective communities, those future westernized but still self-respecting native pioneers were supposed to introduce a major social change in Mexico: to transform masses of Indians into Mexican citizens.

With Independence (1810) the term "Indian" disappeared from the official terminology of Mexican politicians. It continued, however, to be used by all non-Indians, generally in a derogatory way, and neither merciless exploitation of native labour nor verbal abuses and all other types of discrimination were effectively combated. In spite of a pro-Indian national ideology and loud invitations to Mexican citizenship, natives remained "Indians" in independent Mexico, visible mainly as a "social" problem, and generally invisible as humans.

They became more visible to the strata in power under the presidency of Cárdenas and· a strong, though not widespread, Indianistic movement emerged. Those government-connected Indianists, though generally idealistic people, were implementors and followers rather than innovative decision-makers. Some of them (on lower governmental posts, mainly as bilingual rural teachers) were natives themselves, who identified either as "Indians" or as "Mexicans" and occasionally used their old identity as Zapotecs, Mixtecs, Otomies, etc.

In the books from which native children studied in those Indian boarding schools (*internados*), both ancient and contemporary natives were as invisible as they are today, since for the Indian/non-Indian dychotomy, another, "neutral," rural/urban dychotomy was sub-stituted.[11] Unless they learned it (but they learned it rarely) from their parents, native children did not find much in those books either about histories of their tribes and nations or about their contemporary cultures. But at the same time (and this tendency was strengthened with the growth of Indianist policies) they were told that they should "respect their language," and "after acquiring education they should return to their villages in order to help their people." In fact, they were asked to become Mexicans and remain natives at the same time in a country where ethnic groups have never consolidated, and where the cultural model of ethnicity was not available. This was, indeed, an invitation to a most difficult cultural heroism!

Some of the educated natives, as will be shown later, took this invitation to heroism very seriously, and while functioning as Mexican professionals within the national society, continued to identify themselves as members of their respective native groups, to cultivate their languages, and actively help their communities of origin, their native areas or the Indian population in general, usually with great personal sacrifices. Those people overcame, indeed, difficulties rarely encountered on human paths. Most of them had to make their most important decision, that of leaving the village and going to a distant Indian school, between the ages of ten and thirteen. Some of them had to escape against the will of their parents. They walked for days, hungry and lonely through the unknown country to their uncertain destiny. . . .

3. To Be Or Not To Be An Indian

According to several of my "Realist" interviewees, at least 80 percent of the natives who attained a higher education have become Mexicans and "disappeared as Indians." . . . This book is about those who decided not to "disappear" and asserted themselves loudly as "Indians," and it is about those others who after having dissolved into the Mexican society, decided to reassert themselves as "Nahuas."

Volumes have been written and miles of tape have been produced during Indianist congresses and symposiums to determine who should be called "Indian" and who should not in Mexico. According to some criteria there are as many as 30 million Indians in Mexico, according to others, 15 million or less, while one of my "Realist" interviewees estimated the number of Indians in contemporary Mexico as being no more than 3 million. For him and the members of this movement, the experience of extended living in an Indian community, knowledge and continuous use of the native language, and identification with an aboriginal Indian group were the accepted criteria.

If we look at the criteria of other non-organized Mexican natives, census-makers, politicians, Indianists, and anthropologists, we may distinguish at least six categories of "Indians" in contemporary Mexico:

1. Those who live in native corporate communities, speak an aboriginal language, have preserved a substantial part of precolonial culture, and identify themselves as Zapotecs, Mazahuas, Purepéchas, etc.
2. Those who live in native corporate communities, have preserved a substantial part of the precolonial culture, identify themselves as Zapotecs, Nahuas, Mazahuas, etc. but do not speak their aboriginal language.
3. Those who do not live in native corporate communities, have a still substantial part of their precolonial culture, speak their aboriginal language and do identify themselves as Mixtecs, Nahuas, Otomies, etc.
4. Those who do not live in native corporate communities, do not have much of precolonial culture, speak their aboriginal language and identify themselves as Zapotecs, Mazahuas, Nahuas, etc.
5. Those who neither have their precolonial culture nor speak their aboriginal language, never lived in corporate native communities, but nevertheless identify themselves as "Indians."
6. Those who do not identify themselves as Zaoptecs, Nahuas, Otomies, etc., but do have a substantial part of precolonial native culture and live in corporate native communities.

Most of the "Realists" lived generally until early adolescence in their corporate, mostly monolingual, native communities, and did not lose contact with their region after they moved to Mexico City and acquired a higher education. They are fluent in their native languages and identify themselves as "Indians."

Nahua "Utopians," on the other hand, have been, generally, urban people with little or no native community background, with some knowledge of Nahuatl acquired mainly in late adolescence or in adulthood, and with strong identification with their aboriginal culture, somewhat generalized and modernized; which they want to revive in a peacefully restructured Mexico.

Unlike Western European and North American intellectuals of the postindustrial era, Mexican intellectuals rarely if ever suffer from social *anomie* or alienation though they do often suffer from numerous conflicts. They are either truly involved in the affairs of their country or if they do not have a chance to be involved, they are writing, proclaiming and thus diffusing their ideas on the always pressing problems of national unification, social justice for Mexican masses, economic development, broadening of international contacts and threats of economic and political dependence.

Being a good breadwinner or even succesful businessman or professional is never enough for an educated Mexican man. In order to gain the respect of his family and maintain his own self-respect he has to be at least an amateur ideologist offering monolithic or alternative solutions (realistic or not) for all those burning problems of his country. And some type of deep concern with Indians (whether fearful, hostile, sympathetic or enthusiastic) is always among those burning problems.

Like European Catholic intellectuals who depart and then return again to "Mother Church," those native Mexican intellectuals who organized themselves as "Indians" do not always identify as Indians. They join their Indian associations and disappear from them again. They strongly assert themselves as Indians in some periods of their lives and in some milieux, while identifying themselves, or letting themselves to be identified, tacitly or out loud, as Mexicans in other periods of their lives and in other milieux.

Those who, in a given period of life, identify as "Indians" or as "Nahuas" do blame, and accuse of opportunism, those of their friends who "dissolved" into Mexican society. In their more sober moments, however, they reflect about the complexities of their fate instead of prizing loyalty and condemning treachery. They talk about their multiple loyalties, contradictory pressures, their hesitations and their resolutions, and they try above all to identify their goals: the minimalistic, though nevertheless very difficult, goals of achieving social justice for Indians in the case of the "Realists," and maximalistic goals of the revival of Nahua culture and restructuring of Mexican society, in the case of the "Utopians."

PART I: REALISTS

REALISTS

1. Their Origins, Their Work, Their Families

Out of thirteen Indian "Realists" whom I interviewed, as many as eleven came from the groups who in precolonial times had developed high civilizations. I interviewed two Nahuas, three Purepéchas (known also as Tarascos), four Zapotecs, and three Mixtecs. Only two of the interviewed "Realists" were descendants of less civilized groups, Otomies and Popolocas.

Though several of the "Realists" assured me with a modesty typical of Mexican Indians that their ancestors lived not in the centers of their high civilizations but on the uncivilized fringes, some of them possibly could have been remote descendants of their great rulers, priests, poets and scholars, and I could not help wondering what their fate would have been today if their people were not invaded by Spaniards. Though none of them was willing or able to speculate about his precolonial and colonial ancestors, I wondered what those ancestors would have thought about their social movement and whether they would approve or disapprove of their ideas on the place of Indians within Mexican society. Would they see them, as continuing anti-Spanish resistance, consider them skillful diplomats, wise realists involved in the only type of labour on behalf of their people feasible under the circumstances, or would they brand them, maybe as traitors.

With the exception of one who was still a student of the Polytechnic Institute about to graduate as an engineer in a few months, all of them were already well established as professionals. There were three lawyers, among them two anthropologists, four government officials (three of them working in Indian affairs), two teachers, one engineer and one architect. As is often the case in Mexico, not all of them worked in the professions for which they were trained, a fact about which they bitterly complained, even if they were employed as high government officials for instance. They all assumed, apparently, that they should be able make their unique contributions to the well-being of their people through those professions for which they were trained, not apart from them. The government had a duty to help them in assuming such professional roles, they claimed. "Our villages were poor," one of these unlucky "Realists" (employed outside of his profession) told me, "but we were well integrated into our communities. We could have remained useful and happy over there. But tell me, please, why the white government—I mean, Mexican government—seduced us away from our communities? One would assume that this was done so we could do something really important for our people. But if we have no chance to do it, if we cannot even exercize our professions, we fail our people who have been counting on us, and we are cheated, besides, ourselves."

This is a typical attitude among the "Realists." They all want to utilize their professions in the centers where the decisions are made, and no amount of information about non-Indian professionals in Mexico and elsewhere in similar situations can comfort them. Their situation is different, they insist, since the government which "helped them out of the villages" has a duty "to help them in the performance of their highest responsibilities toward their people, who were invaded, physically exterminated (the term they use often), and twice promised the full citizenship in Mexico." Twice—on this, too, they agree—once during the Independence (of 1810), the second time during the 1910 Revolution—"and twice they were deceived." Then the first moment of hope came during the presidency of Lázaro Cárdenas, and now they see "the second moment of hope in their history since President Echaverriá continues the pro-Indian policies of Lázaro Cárdenas . . . " They will not give up their hopes and they will complain and protest until they get a chance to work for their people "not only half-way. . . . "

Of the thirteen interviewed "Realists," only four (three lawyers and one architect) worked independently in their own little firms. It was interesting to note that those independent professionals talked much less about their work than did the others. They seemed to be much more concerned with their sociopolitical labours, performed through their main Indian organization AMPII and numerous smaller organizations they founded. This has been, obviously, the mainstay of their lives and their ambitions were very high.

I asked each of them what he would do if he were elected president of Mexico, and none of them had difficulty identifying with such a role. "The government has been making major mistakes," one of them told me. "I am not a communist myself but I think we could learn much from the communists about long-range planning. Without planning for at least fifteen years ahead not much can be achieved in this country. We also need more emphasis on science. Land was not distributed in a scientific way during the Agrarian Reform and today we suffer from this. In the area of education, more planning, more thinking, more consistency is needed as well. Look for instance at such inconsistencies: rural children who are so poor have to wear school uniforms, while the children from the metropolitan area do not have to. What is the reason for this? Our teachers make politics instead of doing their job . . . they abandon rural schools and go to Mexico City. The Minister of Education should do something about this. He could stop such escapes and demand that teachers go back to their jobs. But, obviously he is afraid. He depends on the votes of those teachers, who are deeply involved in politics. They control him politically, and this is the problem. He is afraid that they may oppose him if he demands that they do their job . . . "

Whether self-employed or not, most of those interviewed appeared to be not only conscientious but often overconscientious about both their work and their pro-Indian activities.

At the time of my interviews the age of these professionals ranged from twenty-four to sixty-one with a median age of about thirty-five, and ten out of the thirteen were married. Most of them (as many as nine) were married, like their great hero, Benito Juarez, to sympathetic mestizo women from middle and upper-middle urban strata, and lived typical middle class lives at home.

About half of the interviewed "Realists" tried to draw their mestizo wives into their Indian milieux and activities, the others did not. All of them seemed to be very conscious of the respective advantages, hardships, doubts and hopes of their particular marital adaptations.

None of the mestizo wives volunteered or was pressed by her husband into becoming an Indian—a choice as open to Mexican mestizos as the choice of becoming Mexican is open to Mexican Indians. None of the men expected his wife to become an Indian. They have been working to achieve social justice for Indian masses but, as some of them formulated it, they would stop identifying as "Indians" as soon as this social justice was achieved. So why should they expect their mestizo wives to become Indians? In fact they could help them much more by being just what they have been—sympathetic Mexicans.

Being realistic, however, they do not assume that social justice for Indians will be achieved through their efforts within one generation. This is why, probably, some of them want so badly for their children to learn their native langauges or become well-acquainted with the areas of their origin. Maybe, they hope that their children will continue their unfinished labour on behalf of the integration of Indians as equals into Mexican society. The best description of the double life pattern developed by those among the "Realists" who choose not to draw their wives into their Indian activities came from a young Purepécha lawyer who, during his childhood, was "aware of the great social injustices in his native village and was at present very much concerned with the improvement of Indian life throughout Mexico."

When I asked him about his wife, he said: "My wife is from here . . . she is very very white . . . very beautiful. We all marry this way. We marry urban women. We marry them for this refinement they have. We marry them for their social class . . . yes . . . " he added after a while, "I took my wife, naturally, to my Purépecha village and she accepts it without question. We also take our children there from time to time but at home we do not talk about the past, and I do not try to teach them Purépecha. The past is accepted but not talked about. You see, with marriage one starts anyway a new life, and it should be this way . . . "

About their parents, they talked very freely and with visible emotion. I did not have to ask any questions. As a rule their fathers initially opposed their going away from their villages. They wanted their sons to stay home and help them with agricultural labours; they were afraid of strange horrors in the distant *internados* and they were afraid of the hardships and defeats which their sons could suffer in the "civilized world." Their mothers, generally, did not have their own opinions, but echoed the anxieties and preoccupations of their husbands. In all cases, however, the parents finally became reconciled to the decisions of their sons. "They respected my decision," "they respected my will, "they knew that I made up my mind"—this is how they described the final consent of their fathers after much opposition and much discussion. Most of the conflicts were finally resolved between the Indian fathers and their sons.

Only occasionally did I detect in my conversation with the "Realists" some reference to unresolved conflicts between father and son. Such references were usually made when discussing "Realists'" Indian identifications. "I myself never had really strong conflicts with my father, such as some others did," one of the "Realists" told me, "and this is why," he reflected, "I do not have any hesitation about my Indian identity. Those who have strong conflicts with their fathers tend to reject their background . . . "

Some of those "others," apparently had a short association with the Movement during their difficult years as students in Mexico City; later, however, "they dissolved into Mexican society . . . "

There are among these individuals such who, apparently, rejected their Indian families to the extent that they would not recognize their own parents if they met them by chance in Mexico City while in the company of their Mexican friends. They would refer to them as "some unknown Indians."

Unlike those despised people, all those I interviewed had maintained continuous contact with their parents, and talked about them with affection and sometimes with admiration. Some parents decided to come to Mexico City to help their sons during the years of their university studies and remained with them. Some sons helped their parents to move to Mexico City after they became established professionals. Most, however, just visited them in their villages whenever they could. They help their families and introduce improvements to the villages whenever possible.

My interviews suggest that the influence of Indian fathers upon the lives of their educated sons was of great importance and is recognized as such by their sons. An Otomie teacher whom I interviewed and a young Purépecha engineer, for instance, had fathers who were agrarian leaders in their area. The father of the Otomie teacher was assassinated during his struggles for distribution of land, and became an Indian hero in his native region. His son, who at the time of his assassination was only twelve years old, inherited both his land and his status in the area and decided to follow in the footsteps of his father. He farmed and taught in a rural school but moved later into full time agrarian politics. He "did not even have time to get married," though he was already forty at the time of this interview. Though he spoke mainly Spanish and his Otomie "was half-forgotten," his identification with Otomies was strong and he appeared to be very proud of his origins.

The father of a young Purepécha engineer, a teacher in a secondary technical school, was also an important community and agrarian leader. He identified himself, apparently, as both a "Mexican nationalist and Purépecha Indian," and his son admired him greatly. Though he did not try to become an agrarian leader himself, he was strongly influenced by both the political beliefs and the outspoken Purépecha identification of his father. "My father taught me much about Purépecha hieroglyphs," he told me, "and he was very well-informed about the origins of our village as well. He spoke in terms of social equality and justice for all. He made many improvements in our village: brought Cultural Missions there and they organized a library and introduced horticulture." Neither his father nor his stepmother opposed his going to the Indian *internado* at the age of thirteen. During his studies, and later as an established professional, he has returned home as often as possible to make all sorts of improvements. Being an electrical engineer he installed electricity in his village, and has been dreaming now about large-scale industrial development which would assure work for the landless Purepéchas from his area. His political beliefs seem to be colored as well by those of his father. He criticizes PRI, the party in power, for not being sufficiently concerned with justice and equality.

The parents of the thirty-five-year-old Mixtec lawyer, born and raised in one of the poorest Mexican regions, Alta Mixtéca, were also among those exceptional parents who did not oppose but helped their children with their education. Three out of five of his siblings died—a rather typical situation among natives of this extremely poor area. His father was, like many Mixtecs from this area, a travelling *marimba* player, exposed to many people and many ideas. His mother was "a very intelligent woman" he added. "Her father had money and educated her: she was a rural teacher and even had her own typewriter! . . . She was always reading a great deal . . . "

When their two sons graduated from Indian school in Oaxaca, their parents liquidated everything and moved to Mexico City "to help their sons with further education." His father started a little grocery store, and he earns money additionally playing in a *marimba* band. He helped his son to get a job as a *marimba* player as well and this is how he supported himself during his years in law school. They all lived together and became "even more Mixtec than they were ever before." They always had only Mixtec friends, and they used to meet frequently to cook Mixtec food and talk about their villages. They formed "a little Mixtec community in spite of the fact that they lived dispersed throughout the city."

The wife of this Mixtec lawyer was a mestizo from Mexico City but "he took her for the honeymoon trip to his land, and she just loved it . . . " he said.

The sacrifices of his parents and their dedication to him and his brother (a medical doctor employed as a pharmacist) influenced him greatly, it seems. "My God, life is not wealth!" he exclaimed. "I will leave nothing to my children except a really good education. And we shall talk to them a great deal about the Mixtec past as soon as they grow a little older."

2. Sketches of Three "Realists"
a. "Licenciado Gisar," Zapotec Lawyer.
Licenciado Gisar, a sixty-one-year-old Zapotec lawyer, has his large office in a dark building in the old colonial section of Mexico City. The staircase is so dark that it was only on my second visit that I noticed a large inscription on his door which read that all inhabitants of the state of Oaxaca had a right to free legal services.

By that time I was sufficiently acquainted with licenciado Gisar to feel free to joke with him. I also knew that Oaxaca, in Southern Mexico, was his native state since he had already talked a great deal with me about his childhood and adolescence, spent partially in his highland village, partially, after his escape from the village, in the capital city of the same name. "Do not tell me, licienciado Gisar," I said, "that you are not charging anything for legal services to the centuries' old enemies of Zapotecs, the Mixtecs of Oaxaca?"

"Well," he said laughing, "it is quite true that wars between Zapotecs and Mixtecs over this or other pieces of communal land are still going on in Oaxaca, but if I could not afford it, I would restrict my help to Zapotecs only, this is right. But you see . . . by now, I can well afford it, so I give free legal service to anybody who lives in Oaxaca, and Mixtecs live there too. I do exactly what is written on my door . . . "

Licenciado Gisar was born and raised in a little Zapotec village in an inaccessible highland area of Oaxaca. This was an area cut off completely from high Zapotec civilization, he told me: his people did not know anything about great Zapotecs of precolonial times; they knew, however, numerous Zapotec legends and were all very proud of the president Benito Juarez, a great Zapotec, born in this area.

His village, isolated from the world by the mountains, had about twelve hundred inhabitants, and his father, like others in the village, had about thirty hectars of rocky mountainous land on which some corn and beans were cultivated. Besides being a farmer his father was also a sandal (*huarache*) maker, and he himself learned this trade in early childhood. He was the youngest of the thirteen children (he had eight brothers and four sisters), and their life was very poor. Whoever could, tried to escape from this village in spite of its community life, beautiful scenery, music and religious ceremonies. Two of his older brothers became rural teachers and left the village. Three of his sisters married out of the village, one of them to a teacher, and one of the brothers moved to another distant community to cultivate coffee. Though they all wore traditional Indian clothes (*camison* and *huaraches*) and spoke only Zapotec among themselves, his parents knew a little Spanish and in order to help their children talked to them only in Spanish when they were small.[1] He learned Zapoteco not from his parents but from other children in the village.

He went to the local school, studied easily and well but he was also very fond of music. "I was very sentimental," he said. "I liked the music of streams, of birds on wind . . . everything was music in the fields. Since music was so important to me, my father bought me a flute (*instrumento de bocilla*) and I became a village musician, playing in the village band during all the ceremonies."

But in spite of such satisfactions he could not see his future in the village. Like Benito Juarez, he, too, felt that he had a different destiny, and did not want to remain a farmer, as his father wanted him to be. He used to go to the mountains, play 'flute,' and reflect about his future. When he was fourteen he had a girlfriend (*novia*) but she soon received a position as a rural teacher and went away to another village. After this event he became even more rebellious, and told his father that he wanted to accomplish something in life, and would rather become a soldier if this was the only way of getting out of the village into the larger world.

His father opposed his plans. The first opportunity to escape occurred when he was sixteen—still before the Indian *internados* were founded by President Cárdenas. His mother was to go to the market in Oaxaca and he asked whether he could accompany her during this long three-day trip on foot, carrying merchandise. After much discussion she finally agreed, suspecting nothing. "When we arrived in the outskirts of Oaxaca and stopped there for a while," he told me, "I took off my *huaraches* (sandals) and put on a pair of shoes which I took with me since I used to wear them in the village for grand occasions. I later sent them home to my brother from Oaxaca, since

I knew that I would never wear them again in my life. . . . My mother cried when she realized I would not return with her . . . "

In Oaxaca he asked his sister who lived there with her husband, a teacher, whether he could remain with them since he wanted to continue his studies and, like Benito Juarez, "do something with his life." He finally convinced them and remained with them in Oaxaca.

With the help of his brother-in-law he prepared himself for an examination and entered *Preparatoria* (Junior College) to prepare himself for a law career, inspired again by his great hero Benito Juarez. During his years in *Preparatoria* and his first year in law school (also in Oaxaca) he had to work very hard to support himself, playing saxophone in an orchestra and working as a waiter in a cafe. Only in the second year of law school did he start earning money by helping "his people" with all sorts of legal problems: he became their representative and this work prepared him very well for his political career. Like Benito Juarez, he too, wanted to combine his education in law with politics, and he has held all sorts of public office throughout his life, aspiring to the highest ones.

During his studies he returned home every year for a vacation, and became a real village spokesman, invited to speak on all sorts of occasions. His father was very pleased and proud.

After graduation from law school he started his practice as a lawyer in Oaxaca. At that time he helped three of his nephews "out of the village" and educated them in Oaxaca. "I was by then a man of independent means," he told me smiling, "and I liked to enjoy myself. I bought a nice house, a car and married a mestizo lady from Oaxaca. I started travelling all over the state to get acquainted with natives and help them."

When I remarked that by marrying a "mestizo lady from Oaxaca" he did again the same as his hero Benito Juarez, he was really startled. "You know, this never occurred to me," he said, "but, indeed, she has exactly the same background as the wife of Benito Juarez. My wife will be very amused," he added.

When he moved eventually to Mexico City, he continued the same activities: a more extensive legal practice (he was legal advisor for a few companies as well), some public offices, and much more intensive Indianist activities since he became one of the key figures in the AMPII, making his office their headquarters. Our interviews were often interrupted by telephone calls, obviously, from the members of the Association, and there were many educated and uneducated

natives, mainly Zapotecs, coming and going from his office or waiting and talking in the office hall.

When I asked licenciado Gisar about his nephews from Oaxaca,
he smiled sadly: "They do not identify anymore as Zapotecs" he said.
"They dissolved into Mexican society, they do not want to be known
as Indians. But I do not blame them for this," he added. "Anybody
can do whatever he pleases. . . . I am a liberal."

His children were all adults at the time of the interviews, and they
were all Mexicans, living upper-middle class lives. "My wife is completely civilized," he said with a mixture of pride and irony. "She
is made of different clay. . . . She is not in the least interested in my
Indianist activities, and I do not speak with her about them. Neither
are the children, with the exception of one daughter, who has slightly
more modern ideas. She graduated in Economics and with her I may
talk about what interests me."

He later gave me a mimeographed lecture which his daughter had
delivered before some seminar in Mexico City. "This may interest
you," he said. "You may learn something new about the composition
of the city population from this paper," and, indeed, I learned much.

b. *"Ingeniero Ruíz" Purépecha architect*

The forty-three-year-old Purépecha architect has a tiny interior work-
shop in a large office building in the old colonial part of Mexico
City. For the last ten years he has been working on his own, and preferred it this way, he said. Before he worked for a large governmental
firm and "inherited" many clients from that period. His clients were
all Mexicans of many different backgrounds. They all assumed, he
said, that he was just one of many Mexican architects. He did not
talk about personal matters with them, and there was no reason to
tell them that he was Purépecha, he explained.

The Purepecha identify of ingeniero Ruíz, was, however, unambig-
uous and outspoken. Two long interviews which I had with him were
interrupted several times by various Purépecha friends who dropped
by for a while to visit him. He spoke with them Purépecha. "This is
the most beautiful language," he remarked to me, "a language well
worth fighting for. . . . One sings rather than speaks in this language."

Ingeniero Ruíz spoke easily and with obvious pleasure about his
childhood and about his activities within the Indianist Movement.
He looked and acted much younger than his age, a tall, slim man
with lively gestures. He excused me for the interruptions but his
office was "a contact point for many Purépechas" he said. "This was

the easiest place to meet for discussions about their problems and plans connected with their work in a Purépecha region."

He was born and stayed until the age of ten in a little Purépecha village with about fifteen hundred inhabitants, located around sixty kilometers from Lake Pazcuaro, the central point of the old Purépecha lands. This was a bilingual village, he said, a very poor village, which was made even more miserable after Agrarian Reform since the agrarian officials "took over communal lands for themselves, as a payment for all they did for the Mexican Revolution," he added with irony.

At the time he was a child there were no large properties in his village. "We all had communal lands and little private lots of about two hectars per family." The people in his village were "very conscious of their precolonial history, without knowing the details." They knew that "among their forefathers there was much more equality, decency, desire to work hard and well; more compassion and mutual respect." Everybody knew as well, he added, "that in precolonial times we formed a larger, extra-local entity."

He was the eldest son in his family of three boys and two girls. Being the eldest one he had to help his father in the fields, and since his early childhood he was well aware of the miserable economic situation and of his helplessness, since the work was too hard and he could not really help his father. He reflected a great deal on how to get out of the village.

The opportunity occurred at the time he was ten years old, when his older cousin, who worked in Cultural Missions, came to visit them. They went together to the stream and talked for a long time. He learned from his cousin about Indian *internados*, organized by President Lázaro Cárdenas, and begged him to take him away so he could educate himself. His parents strongly opposed this idea "but when they realized how determined I was, they finally agreed." He left together with his cousin and they walked for three days to a rural *internado* in the state of Puebla. This was at first a coeducational school; soon however, it was changed into an all-male *internado* for about 340 boys of various aboriginal groups. They all lived together in large dormitories of 42 boys each, worked in the fields for several hours per day, and at the end of every year the remaining products were divided among them. They had to cook for themselves and they studied in the same *internado* in which they lived. Besides several dormitories and the kitchen, the *internado* had a large dining room, library and even a theater for all sorts of functions. Teachers, who also lived in the *internado*, though in separate rooms, were all bilingual, but since he was the only Purepécha, there was no bilingual Purépecha teacher in this *internado*. Most of the boys were Totonoca, Popoloca, Chontoles and Otomies, but among themselves they spoke Spanish. "But since I hardly knew any Spanish, I had to learn first Totonoca from the boys in order to study later in Spanish with a Totonoca bilingual teacher," he added smiling. "It took me one year to adapt," he said. "After a year I, too, could speak Spanish. But do not think that I forgot my Purépecha language during my years in *internado*," he continued. "It is a lie that one can forget one's native language . . . I used to write letters to my parents, and I visited my cousin who lived about forty kilometers from the *internado* and we talked and talked Purépecha. . . . In fact I improved my native language during those years, though I spoke Spanish only in the internado . . . " he ended with obvious satisfaction.

After three years he returned for the first time to his village and remained for two months' vacation. His parents were, apparently, so pleased with him that they insisted that he should go ahead with his studies. "Father did not even put me to work," he said, "but I, naturally, volunteered myself."

After he graduated from the *internado* he went to Mexico City where he had some friends from the village who were studying in the Polytechnic Institute. He was always interested in drawing (in the *internado* they all had learned some trade and he was a skilled furniture-maker), "so it occurred to me that I could, maybe, study architecture." He graduated from the Polytechnic Institute as an architect, earning his living, as did other Purépecha boys, as a designer. "We all helped each other and stayed together during our studies," he added.

He was married early to a mestizo woman from Mexico City and by the time I interviewed him, he had adolescent sons, one of them a student of *Preparatoria*.

Though his Indianist activities probably diminished, as is usually the case, during the first, most difficult, years of his professional career, by the time I met him, he was again deeply involved with them. He was not only active as a member of Mexican Association of Indigenous Professionals and Intellectuals (AMPII) but was also a leader of a Purépecha group designed to help the people from his region. This was a particularly dynamic group since, as he told me, as many as thirty-eight professionals came out of his little village, and most of them remained in Mexico City. "We all owe our successes to President Lázaro Cárdenas," he insisted throughout both interviews. "This great man not only founded the *internados* for us but he forced our parents to send us to local schools when we were small, as well. He imposed fines on those parents who would not send their children to schools, and this did really help since the law was strongly enforced during the times of his presidency."

Ingeniero Ruíz maintains contact with his family and his village mainly through his Indianist activities since he goes to the region as often as he can together with his friends to mediate between the village and various offices, to fight exploitation, and to introduce progress.

He helped his brother "out of the village" and gave him the only job he could in his little firm. This was the job of foreman, and his brother resents this subordinate position a little. "This was his fault, however," ingeniero Ruíz assured me. "He had the same chance to get an education as I did but he was afraid to try."

His wife, he said "did not speak Purépecha yet, and she was quite distressed about it" since all their friends have been Purepécha, and speak this language at their social gatherings at home. "But there was so little time to help her with learning the language," he added. "Our children, however," he said proudly, "already begin to speak Purépecha." This I checked myself when I met his eldest son who came to the father's office and talked for a while with his Purépecha friends.

c. "Señor Gonzalez," Teacher, Government Official, Student of Anthropology.

I interviewed Señor Gonzalez in a large modern governmental office where he was employed in a section of Indian Affairs. Our interviews took place in a large room with numerous desks, in the early morning before working office hours, and late, around seven or eight p.m., when everybody had left.

Señor Gonzalez, a young man of twenty-six, made it very clear from the start that his role as a minor government official was only one of his multiple social roles. He was trained as a rural teacher and for his young age had, indeed, a great deal of experience as a school inspector among rural Indians. His involvement in the Indianist movement was only marginal since, in spite of his striking modesty, his ambitions were very high. His not-yet-crystallized sociopolitical dreams were postponed for after his graduation from the School of Anthropology. Through those studies he wanted to learn about the prehistory of his group and about Mexican natives in general. Though he was very busy with his office work and already married.

he spent all of his evenings as a part-time student in the School of Anthropology. His scholarly ambitions were striking but he confessed that his difficulties were enormous. He was still thinking predominantly in Nahuatl, he said, as his Spanish vocabulary was not yet adequate and from time to time he missed some parts of the lectures.

He was born and raised in a small Nahua village of 680 inhabitants in a tropical area. He had three sisters and two brothers, of whom he was the eldest—"and this meant to be really chained . . . " he commented, with some hesitation since he had told me already about his deep attachment to his family. This was an isolated, purely Nahua, village, organized since 1938 as *ejido*, governed by mostly monolingual Nahuas, with only three mestizo officials. Practically everybody was monolingual, and all adults still wear today the regional native clothes in this village. Some old Indian customs are still practiced on the occasions of planting and harvest, "but only current Catholic images are evoked during those ancient Nahua ceremonies, though we do not even have a church in our little village," he added reflectively. "There is no church, no patron saint, and people do not have the custom of church-going. Only once in a while the priest is called to bless a newly built house, to celebrate a *fiesta* or marry a couple. We have to pay very much for such services."

Señor Gonzalez did not learn anything about Aztec civilization in his village. He did not even know that his people had had such a high culture in the past. "The social memory of my people was restricted to dwelling on our marginality," he reflected, "our marginality, and the horrors and tortures of the times of *hacienda* (pre-colonial and pre-Agrarian-Reform era). . . . "

He learned some Spanish as a child and went to rural school in his area. Neither in school, however, nor later in an Indian *internado* did he learn the truth about his ancestors, since Spanish-speaking teachers imposed mestizo values upon children and described Aztecs to them as being "primitive people." He never had a bilingual teacher, and the mestizo teachers "talked to us mainly about the times of Independence and about equal rights for all Mexicans," he said. "This education was so contradictory to our reality, however. . . . The county, for instance, would charge us as much as 100 pesos for every birth certificate, and you know well what it meant for the people who were so poor." (I was certainly well aware of what it meant. In the Mazahua village where I worked in the 1960s it was hard for a Mazahua Indian to earn eight pesos for a day's work.)

In spite of such a restricted and hopeless life there were strong social controls which kept everybody in the village. Those who tried to get out were branded as "lazy"—good men were supposed to work hard and stay forever in their community.

"My father," said señor Gonzalez, "was very different, however. He was uneducated and very modest but had much broader, really philosophical, ideas. He felt that his sons should all become educated and accomplish something in life. We talked with him a great deal and he would always give us moral support. This is why all his sons acquired education. No, my sisters did not get educated," he added, "since at those times it was just unthinkable for a girl to go away from the village."

At the age of sixteen he managed to leave the village and go to the Indian *internado* from which he graduated in one year and returned again to his village in order to help his father. Though his parents badly wanted him to go ahead with his education, he knew that they needed his help and felt obliged to stay in the village. "And in spite of all my ambitions," he said, "I lasted this way for the whole three years, and then my younger brothers would return also one by one to help us with work."

But one day when he learned from a classmate that special courses for graduates of *internados* were being organized in the state of Puebla, he decided to leave and finish a two months' course for *Promotores Culturales* (cultural leaders). He had very good luck in having an old professor, a woman-anthropologist, "who had discovered something good in me," he said, "and gave me much encouragement and help. I owe so much to her. She helped me later to get this job in Mexico City and persuaded me to study anthropology as well. . . . She is already retired but lives in Mexico City, so I can see her from time to time. She always believed in me . . . "

This development came about through a paper which Mr. Gonzalez wrote after a period of collective field work, during his studies in the state of Puebla. This was a paper on commercial activities at the rural market. "My paper really pleased my teacher," he said, "and this has shaped my fate as you see . . . "

After he finished a two months' course for *Promotores Culturales*, Mr. Gonzalez along with other graduates entered the *Instituto Federal de Capacitación de Magisterio* (Teachers' College) in Jalapa, state of Veracruz, and spent six years there studying and working at the same time as a school inspector in his native area. While in Jalapa he lived with other classmates in a special house for *Promotores Culturales*. While in the field as a school inspector he had the opportunity to continue his studies through correspondence courses. Throughout his studies he maintained contact with his parents returning as often as he could to his village.

"Now when I live in Mexico," he said, "I go there even more frequently. We have really nice family gatherings in the village and we talk with my father for hours. We helped him naturally and his life is just completely different by now. . . . I would like eventually to move into a Nahua area," he added. His wife was a mestizo from Mexico City, "but she would have to learn Nahuatl," he said, "since we are going to live there after I graduate from the School of Anthropology."

3. Out of the Village

The establishment of an economically sound and humane relationship between antiquated agriculture and increasingly centralized modern industry is a difficult problem for which no adequate solution is so far available.

The influx of an unskilled and helpless rural population into the cities, and particularly the capital, has been recently identified as one of the great national problems in Mexico. It is hard to estimate the percentage of natives among those rural immigrants to the cities.[2] The "Realists" whom I interviewed were acutely aware of this unsolved and painful problem. They generally believed that the rural natives would have preferred, if possible, to remain in their villages. Their Movement concentrated much of its efforts on the improvement of living conditions, agricultural, technical and social, in the Indian villages. At the same time, however, they claim that some natives, the most ambitious and talented, should leave their villages (as they did), acquire higher education and try to help their people from the power centers in Mexico City. And they deplore the fact that some natives who left villages and acquired higher education forgot about their responsibilities toward their regions and "dissolved into Mexican society."

Interviews with the thirteen "Realists" suggest that there have been powerful social forces pushing the natives out of their villages. Extreme poverty, acute rural unemployment and a feeling of hopelessness have been, probably, the most important among them, while the population explosion, so emphasized by students of underdeveloped or developing nations, has hardly affected the areas in which they were born.[3] This poverty and hopelessness has been greatly increased, it seems, through all sorts of village "parasitism."[4] All of the interviewed "Realists" spoke of such rural "parasites." Village *caciques*, both mestizos and Indians, merchants, labor recruiters, priests, politicians were among the most often mentioned "parasites"[5] who have been trying to gain power, money and glory at the expense of the native population.

But my interviews suggest as well the presence of different forces strongly attracting the young natives to urban centers, particularly to Mexico City. The most often mentioned among those attractive forces were the visits of already "civilized" relatives, as well as the influence of other people from "the larger world," such as rural teachers, merchants and "cultural missionaries,"[6] who often unwillingly contributed to the growth of a "city mystique" among the youth of native villages. The tales about great opportunities in Mexico City and about the rights of all natives to full Mexican citizenship (available as they assumed mainly in the urban centers) came to them generally through such personal contacts and through occasional exposure to political discourses of campaigning politicians.

The great "journeys to civilization" (as they were termed by the interviewed "Realists") were made, so to speak, in two giant steps: 1) the difficult exit from the village to an *internado*, Indian boarding school, generally located either in a distant rural area or in a small town, and 2) another courageous jump from the *internado* to Mexico City in search of higher education.

Both of those giant steps required courageous, often heroic, decisions with great traumatic consequences.

Most of those I interviewed were forbidden to go to "those dangerous schools where Indian children were fattened for oil for Russian planes."[7] The opposition of land owners, merchants and clergy to this Cárdenas-inspired "socialistic education" for natives was very strong and it continued in many rural areas long after his presidency was over.

Like the little Zapotec shepherd, Benito Juarez, who later became a Mexican president, most of the interviewed "Realists" had some contacts either in the town or in the *internado* to which they went against the protests or with the reluctant consent of their parents. They were usually helped by an older brother, married sister, teacher, cousin, friend, or even local politician. All those lucky individuals who "had already made it" felt obliged to help those courageous young boys.

The memories of those adventurous expeditions were greatly idealized, and I would say even "formalized," by those I interviewed. I had

to press them for concrete details on their often truly spectacular
"escapes" from their villages. Unlike uneducated natives who often
have a real obsession with empirical truth, those native professionals,
however strong their Indian identification, used the abstract and
vague language, so typical of the first generation of educated village
mestizos,[8] while telling me about their adventures. They were, however, quite precise and matter-of-fact relating the less glamorous
events.

To my question, "Please tell me how did you get out of the villlage
and acquire an education?" many of them would answer, for instance:
"I did it through my strong will . . . through my aspiration toward
something better . . . through my desire to perfect myself . . ." And
they responded with a certain disbelief, and some sense of humilia-
tion, when I asked them whether they took a bus, a train or whether
they walked, how long and with whom, from where they got money
for a ticket, what they ate during their journeys and where they slept.

Only after they answered, with some reluctance, such down-to-earth
questions, would I come back to their most important image of their
"great escapes to civilization," since this is generally how they see it,
whatever importance they attach to their own precolonial civilizations. Some of them told me sadly that their great civilizations were
destroyed and reduced to "hardly perceivable," "hard to admire" and
"often harmful customs." So now, they assumed, the only realistic
adaptation left to them was to absorb the occidental civilization in
its Mexican version as fully as possible. They would like to do it,
however, without destroying what was most valuable in their past.
According to them the most valuable elements of their native traditions are not specific customs and beliefs but the traditional precolonial
morality which had survived in some Indian villages. The essential
ingredients of this morality are, according to one of the "Realists,"
1. communal spirit, higher, less egotistic and more socially constructive than modern Mexican individualism; 2. strong family ties and,
particularly, great respect and responsibility toward the parents and
elders in general; and 3. veracity: Indians take their word of honor
much more seriously than do Mexicans. They never break their word
and keep their commitments sometimes through generations. These
qualities they would like not only to retain—as I heard from many
"Realists"—but to incorporate into Mexican life as well.

The second giant step was from the primary and sometimes secondary schools (most of them Indian *internados*) to Mexico City in search
of further educational opportunities. The idea behind Indian *inter-*

nados was to create educated native leaders who would return to their villages and help their people with community development. But Indian *internados* were, usually, far away from the home villages of their pupils, and this prevented their anticipated continuous contact. Some of my interviewees told me that they returned home only once per year for vacation; others did not return for two or three years. A few from among them returned home after their graduation from the *internado* for several months or even for a couple of years to help their fathers with agricultural work; none of them returned for good in order to become an Indian leader.

Though all of the "Realists" whom I interviewed became dedicated to sociopolitical work on behalf of Indian communities, they all claimed that this work had to be done in the center of the country, "where all decisions are made," (quite a realistic estimate of Mexican political centralism), not from within their local communities. They were taught in the *internados* that they had the right to full Mexican citizenship, and they were told over and over again that they should respect their origins and work for their people. They decided to do it in the most rational, most efficient way, through participation in all decisions concerning Indians. And these decisions, as all important decisions in this highly centralized republic, are made in the capital, Mexico City.

Guidance must have failed in another area as well in those Indian *internados*. Their graduates, though invited to full citizenship, were not fully informed about available careers through which they could work for the economic development of their areas, for full citizenship of Indian masses, for more effective educational opportunities, for the physical well-being of natives and for their freedom from severe conflicts, both exterior and interior. They did not know about the possibilities of becoming economists, anthropologists, psychologists, food technologists or many other careers. It was assumed that they would become rural teachers and would not aspire to other occupational roles.

Occupational choice among my interviewees was much more diversified, however. No social milieu is completely closed in our times, and even without adequate vocational guidance the Indian boys from *internados* learned about the existence of other professions. Three of them chose, like Benito Juarez, to become lawyers, three out of the thirteen interviewed became engineers, and all of those, with one exception, who continued their education in colleges for rural teachers managed to move eventually to Mexico City, and at the time of this research were employed by the federal bureaucracy, mainly in departments devoted to Indian education. My interview data suggests that in the case of an occupation less well known than that of lawyer, teacher and engineer, there always existed some special stimulus, some exposure to the previously unknown profession, or some encouragement on the part of such a professional.

About their first months in Mexico City they all talked with a certain reluctance, returning to their idealized exits from the villages and to the description of their current involvements in Indianist activities, of which they were, obviously, very proud. It seemed as if those first difficult but hardly glamorous steps in the capital were somehow clouded in their memories, squeezed between the sharply remembered childhood years and the recent professional and Indianist accomplishments.

A forty-eight-year-old Popoloca employed in one of the city institutions as an archivist after graduation from an Indian *internado* at the age of eighteen returned for vacations to his village in order to help his father in the fields. By then, however, his parents were already convinced that he should go ahead with his secondary studies to acquire further education and establish himself as a professional.

With their encouragement but without knowing anybody in Mexico City, he decided to take a bus to the capital. He checked into a little hotel, and started searching for his classmates from the *internado* in various secondary schools. Finally he located one of them and this boy helped him to enter a secondary-level Indian *internado* in Mexico City, "also founded by General Cárdenas." He graduated from this *internado* at the age of twenty-two, and after some searching found a job as an assistant office clerk, so he could maintain himself during his evening professional studies in the School of Commerce. He lived miserably with his Indian friends from the *internado*. They cooked together and helped each other in everything. He worked from seven a.m. until three p.m. in his office, returned home for dinner, then from six until nine p.m., he went to evening classes. This was a very hard life—he had to study at night or during his work in the office, and often went practically the whole day without eating since he earned so little and his friends did not earn much either.

A thirty-year-old Purépecha electrical engineer from a younger generation of Movement intellectuals lived in Mexico City with relatives and during his secondary level studies he too had to work very hard. From eight to five, he worked installing mosaic floors and then attended night school every evening. During his university years in the Polytechnic Institute his work was better paid since he found a job with the City Public Works. This work too was very absorbing and harmful to his studies. "In spite of those hardships, however, I had such high spirits, believe me, very high spirits indeed, during all those difficult years . . ." he confessed. "I knew that my father wanted me to succeed and this meant so much to me—and I was fascinated with my studies. . . . I selected electrical engineering since this was so completely unknown and mysterious to me and I love my career."

Many of the "Realists" mentioned the American anthropologist, Oscar Lewis's books on the culture of poverty in Mexico City. Unlike Mexican professionals, so often highly critical of and indignant about his "biased findings," several of those interviewed defended Oscar Lewis's books without identifying themselves, generally, with the "Sanchez Family" and other characters. Only one of them, a thirty-two-year-old Purépecha lawyer told me without further elaboration of these obviously painful memories, "I always do defend Oscar Lewis since I myself did live the life of the Sanchez family . . ." but then on the occasion of another interview he added, "My life in the village was even more similar to that of Sanchez family than my life in Mexico. . . . There are so many people in Mexico City and one cannot die here from hunger. But in the village the unemployment was so acute that we suffered terrible hunger. We could not even buy *huaraches* (sandals) sometimes, and our feet would bleed when we worked in the field. And we had to hire ourselves to work for mestizos—there were about 20 percent of them in our village, and believe me, they really made you suffer. . . . But . . ." he added after a while, "I have to admit that the natives to whom we had to hire ourselves made us suffer as well. . . ."

After the conversations about this period of their lives it became clear to me that those ambitious and courageous men had faced the great danger of dropping into the hopeless city marginality during their first months and sometimes even first years in the capital. They all succeeded in overcoming this terrible danger. Their thirst for "something better" their feeling of responsibility toward those left behind in the villages, their determination to "do something in life," their mutual help for one another during those times of hardship, and finally their membership in the AMPII, the Movement which grew out of their first years in Mexico City—all those factors helped them to fight for their place in Mexican life, and for the "civilization" they wanted to acquire so badly.

4. Life Cycle of the Movement

At the time of my research (spring summer, 1973) the Movement's main organization AMPII was already twenty-five years old and its core members were already well-established middle-aged professionals. Around this main organization circulated a variety of submovements with similar ideologies but of a regional, not metropolitan, character.

Like many movements, this one as well had its cherished prehistory. This prehistory consisted of informal gatherings of the graduates of Indian *internados*, young men of similar background, under the leadership of a Zapotec student of anthropology, an exceptionally energetic young man with broader contacts and larger horizons. Out of those informal gatherings emerged the first formal organization headed by the same energetic young leader. This organization was called *Confederacion Nacional de Jovenes y Comunidaded Indigenas* (National Confederation of Indigenous Youth and Indigenous Communities). The members of this organization wanted to maintain contacts among themselves, to help each other during their studies, and to organize an effective vechicle to help their communities of origin.

In 1948 when some of the founders received their higher education credentials and others were nearing this objective, the Mexican Association of Indigenous Professionals and Intellectuals (AMPII) was formed, and the Movement started to grow.

Three stages can be distinguished in the life-cycle of this Movement: 1) the movement's consolidation, characterized by great enthusiasm from its founders and first members; 2) a weakening of the movement due mainly to the great difficulties with which the young native professionals were confronted in the first period of their careers; 3) the revitalization of the movement at the time when its founders were well established in their careers, and had more time to devote to their Indianist activities.

These stages of the Movement correspond roughly to the "social ages" of its members. The Movement consolidated during the youth of its founders at the time when they were students, most of them still single, in need of each other's help. They often lived together in order to lessen living costs and cooperate more effectively.

The weakening of the Movement corresponds to their adulthood, to the pressures from their new families, new careers, and their first uncertain successes. Their fathers' hopes, their own pride, even the future of the Movement, all depended on their establishing them-

selves as professionals, a very difficult struggle for men without contacts, and with such great responsibilities toward "those left behind."

The revitalization of the Movement occurred when its founders
reached middle age and were already secure in their positions, had
more contacts and more time for their Indianist activities.

Though designed from the beginning as an open movement, and
accepting constantly new, younger members, the Movement at the
time of my research was mainly run by its pioneers, particularly the
Movement's founder and dynamic leader, Zapotec anthropologist
"señor Barrios Ortega," chief of a governmental department devoted
neither to anthropology, nor to Indian affairs. All my interviewees
talked very highly of this man, who had a similar background as other
native professionals but a much broader vision and larger contacts.
Some of the younger members still struggling to establish themselves
in their careers told me that they remained in the Movement in spite
of a lack of time and energy only because of the high respect and
friendship they felt for "señor Barrios Ortega." Some others from
among the younger members had, obviously, their own leadership
ambitions, and without drifting away from the original Movement,
began to be more active in small regionally oriented submovements
which they organized themselves. Those submovements, usually
called "regional committees," have been mostly single-native group
movements, and are devoted to helping people "left behind" in the
villages or regions of their leaders. Nahuas, Mixtecs, Zapotecs,
Purepéchas all had such auxiliary submovements, some quite large,
such as one Mixtec organization with six hundred members.

Though from one point of view the emergence of this Movement
may be seen as an attempt by native students to help each other in
an unknown, dangerous capital, the Movement would probably
not have emerged if a certain special sociopolitical climate had not
existed at that time in Mexico.

This was a time of great economic and ideological excitement, the
beginning of the spectacular post-World War II economic growth
which some contemporary economists call today "growth without
development."[9] But at that time neither the privileged nor the underprivileged strata were conscious of the dangers of such an economic
boom. Whoever could, tried to join it and to be as close as possible to
the centers of economic decisions.

Since in Mexico no major development in the area of public life
occurs without ideology, this was also a period of revival of the rather
fossilized ideology of the Mexican Revolution, an attempt to supple-

ment its egalitarian ideals through the slogan of "economic resources
for all." This was an era of reemphasis on unification of the country,
a time of new nationalistic self-assertions. This self-confident, economically flavored nationalism was based, however, on the incorrect
assumption that most of the Indians were already acculturated and
integrated in one way or another, and that those who were not, were
given a realistic opportunity for painless integration.

After describing his first most difficult steps in Mexico City, the
forty-eight-year-old Popoloca archivist told me that his life changed
completely after "his fate made him encounter "professor Barrios
Ortega," the founder of the Movement, during one of the reunions
among graduates of Indian *internados.*" He was invited to join the
Movement and with great nostalgia described "the high ideals we had
to help our people to progress. Later, however," he added, "we all
acquired different professions, and it was more and more difficult to
meet and less and less time to work together . . ."

The revival of the movement, most of them insisted, was greatly
influenced by the election of President Luis Echaverriá Alvarez in
1970. This was due not only to the Indianist policies of this president,
whom the members of the movement described as a "follower of the
President Lázaro Cárdenas," but to President Echaverriá's years-long
acquaintance with the Movement's founder, "Professor Barrios
Ortega." ("Professor Barrios Ortega" in his youth had joined a
governmental party PRI and there became acquainted with Luis
Echaverriá Alvarez, the active and influential member with strong
Indianist sympathies.) Though "Professor Barrios Ortega" did not, as
he assured me, take advantage of this high contact ("and even if he
wanted, he could not since the president was too busy") everybody in
the Movement knew about this personal contact, and this knowledge
certainly gave a new boost to the morale of the Movement.

Even those from among the "Realists" whose political orientations
were closer to democratic socialism than to the laissez faire capitalism
endorsed by the governmental party, had good words to say about
the Indianist policies of President Echaverriá. "Now with Mr. Echaverriá the government says to the natives: *Do not give up!*" commented the forty-three-year-old Purépecha architect. "His government
gave jobs to those educated natives who still spoke their native languages. . . . They received jobs in units specializing in Indian affairs,
and that is how he won our confidence. . . . If there is any future
for us, it lies in the integration of real natives into national affairs.
. . . They should be aware of the country's problems. Our natives

lack self-confidence . . . they do not know how to defend themselves. When they gain self-confidence they will know how to assert
themselves. . . . Our people when awakened can be very rebellious . . . "

5. Social Structure of the Movement

Like many new, dynamic social movements, the movement of the
Mexican Indian "Realists" has a core organization and a number of
satellite organizations which share its main purpose and ideology
but usually have their own leadership and their own style of action.
Unlike the core organization AMPII the membership of those satellite
organizations is not restricted to natives with higher education. They
are usually one-native-group organizations or even one-region and
sometimes only one-village organizations. The leaders of those satellite organizations (most of them either current or ex-members of
AMPII) are usually younger than AMPII leaders, and they seem to
be slightly more left-wing politically, without obvious communist
sympathies, however. In several important ways those organizations
are structurally similar to AMPII whatever their deviations, disagree-
ments and separate aspirations may be:

1. They operate on the same two levels (a) they provide the place
   for interchange of ideas, favors, contacts among their members;
   (b) they are dedicated to helping the Indian masses with whom
   they maintain continuous contact.
2. They strongly emphasize national scale lobbying activities on
   behalf of the Indian masses and try to place their members in
   positions of power.
3. Their strategies are reformist and revisionistic rather than
   revolutionary.

The formal organization of AMPII and of its satellite organizations
is modeled on a Mexican (or more generally European) type of voluntary organization. The association has its secretary-general, secretary
in charge of planning, its treasurer (called "secretary of finances") and
its legal advisor. Its headquarters are at present in the large private
office of one of the AMPII's prominent members.

Membership in the Movement was estimated by its founder as fluctuating between four hundred and five thousand, those numbers being
an estimate of the active members within the whole Mexican Republic
during the Movement's duration. Such data are, naturally, only rough

approximations since, unlike the membership of smaller and less dynamic voluntary organizations, the membership of social movements can rarely be estimated with accuracy. Those fluctuations have been, apparently, a function of two main factors: 1) stronger or weaker demands on the time of the Movement's members connected with their age, family responsibilities, and demands of their professional careers and 2) the tendency of the Movement's members to "dissolve into Mexican society," and to return again to the Movement under the influence of various personal, national or even international occurrences.

AMPII publishes two periodicals (neither of them appearing regularly) and occasional pamphlets. Those two periodicals reflect the double function of the movement:

1. *Cuadernos del AMPII* (Notebooks of AMPII) is a platform for educated Indians, directed mainly toward Mexican power elites.
2. *La Voz del Indio* (Voice of the Indian) is a popular publication meant to inform the Indian masses about what has been done on their behalf by AMPII and transmit to the Mexican Government and Mexican elites the problems of the Indian masses as perceived by those people themselves.

Though AMPII's founder has been connected with the party in power, PRI, and other members profess a variety of political creeds, the organization has remained politically independent. I was told by several of those interviewed that the Movement's political independence was, apparently, like most other decisions, a result of long discussions and carefully weighed arguments among the members rather than of the emotional predilection of the leaders. I noted the same emphasis on political independence, and the same rationalistic style of arriving at common decisions, among the members of "satellite organizations" as well. They did not want, they insisted, to deviate from their main objective, that of bringing social justice to the Indian masses, and this is why they did not want to associate themselves as a Movement with any political party. They would not accept any governmental subsidies either since this could alter their main objectives.

To qualify for membership in AMPII one has to have either a diploma from an institution of higher learning (University, Polytechnics or other type of higher professional school) or to be active as an intellectual, a writer, artist, journalist, etc.

Among older AMPII members, however, are some who finished

vocational schools only, and some others who started but did not complete their higher education. The criterion of higher education seems, indeed, less important than other requirements for membership. Among them the most important are: 1) the members had to have been born in Indian communities of Indian parents, 2) they have to speak a native language, and 3) they have to have an Indian identification.

Formal entrance to the AMPII is secured through the presentation of a lecture on some Indian-related theme; this requirement has not been, however, strongly enforced.

Identification has been considered, probably, the most important of those requirements, and it has been defined in terms of pro-Indian activities rather than in terms of pro-Indian self-assertions or "inner feelings," which, as some of the "Realists" admitted, may be quite fluctuating or ambivalent. There is an oath which every member of AMPII has to take, in which he promises that he will always defend his fellow-Indians against prejudice and injustice. If a member of the Association fails to protect another Indian (out of bad will, pressure or conflict) some sort of a trial is organized and he may be deprived of membership. Such an expulsion does not mean, however, a complete ostracism. It means, rather, redefinition of the relationship with the expelled member, while the family or friendship bonds (only in a slightly modified form) may continue forever between the expellers and the expelled. Such an attitude may mean either flexibility of ideology or great tolerance. On the basis of my interviews with "Realists" I am rather inclined to think that it is due to tolerance, based on the recognition of the exceptionally strong pressures and exceptionally difficult situations with which Indian professionals and intellectuals are confronted when they try to defend (often against the whole society) their unjustly treated fellow-Indians. It is assumed that such difficulties are too hard on an average human being, however decent he may be. He is, therefore, allowed to continue his non-heroic but nevertheless difficult life, since not everybody—they realistically assume—is born for heroism.

If we define "heroism" (a term Indian "Realists" never use since they speak rather in terms of "duty" and "decency") as surpassing of positive norms required by a given society in a situation of continous pressure, conflicts and dangers—then we may say, indeed, that heroic attitudes and actions are definitely required from the members of the Movement, who do not expect, however, the same heroism from other educated Mexican natives.

6. Ideology and Strategies

The ideology of the Movement is expressed without overstatement or grandiose promises in *Cuadernos del AMPII* (Notebooks of AMPII), *Voz del Indio* (Voice of the Indian) and other occasional publications of the association.

In all the activities of "Realists" as well as in their periodicals two themes are constant: 1) the goal of influencing Mexican society (mainly the federal government and, to a lesser degree, state governments) by presenting them with new and correct data on contemporary Indians, and protesting incorrect data and formulations on Indian conditions; and by interpreting the demands of noneducated Indians which may be misunderstood by the federal and state authorities. (Such activities have been also carried out through occasional pamphlets, lectures, round-tables, articles in the national press, television appearances, participation in congresses and various ad hoc groups which try to pressure the federal government and influence public opinion.) 2) the goal of mediation between Indian communities and "the larger world": local non-Indian areas and agencies of federal and state governments.

These Indian "Realists" often organize themselves into field-groups modeled on Cultural Missions from the time of Cárdenas. These field-groups consist usually of several professionals: doctors, lawyers, teachers, engineers, who travel to various Indian communities trying to help them with "integral development." This is understood as technological and educational progress, explained to village Indians and implemented in such a way that it becomes compatible with traditional native values and is accepted without reservation.

The activities in which most of the members are involved require indeed more courage, persistence and moral strength than those performed by the Cultural Missions which had behind them the support and protection of the Mexican Government. Conflicts with the existing structures and hostility from the non-Indian local population and from various Indian *caciques* as well are very great, and some of the interviewed "Realists" told me that many such self-appointed "cultural missionaries" barely escaped with their lives while on expeditions to remote rural areas.

The vision of a better future for Indians is identified in these publications with the vision of a better future for the Mexican Republic and presented as a continuation of the "half-forgotten" (as is often stressed) ideology of the Mexican Revolution. "We would like to implement the concepts of the Mexican Constitution," said one of my interviewees, "the concept that we are all equal. We want to integrate our people into national life, but," he added, "the Indian concepts should also have influence on national life . . ." When I asked him what specific Indian characteristics should influence Mexican national life, he had a ready answer. "For instance the Indian concept of honor," he said, "and the sense of community, the joy we derive from helping one another."

The motto of the AMPII, printed on the front page of every issue of *Cuadernos*, is "Let's Mexicanize Indians, not Indianize Mexico!" For the majority of Mexicans this motto means "the integration of the Indian population into national society," a phrase to which several generations of post-revolutionary Mexicans became so accustomed that they have almost stopped perceiving its significance. But this motto for the "Realists" means much more than an attempt at integration of Indians into national society. This integration must occur with a minimum of suffering of Indian masses, without loss of the natives' sense of dignity and with maximum preservation of their indigenous cultures. It is essential—claim the Indian "Realists"—that the implementation of this program be carried out under the leadership of educated natives who, like themselves, came out of a truly Indian milieu, understand their people, and can have their confidence.

This is a strong and controversial statement, though it may not appear to be such. A great majority of the Indianist scholars and activists in Mexico do not qualify as "educated natives." This statement, though formulated in the customarily quiet manner of these Indian "Realists" in fact strongly challenges the governmental policies of INI (*Instituto Nacional Indigenista*, National Indianist Institute) and its social composition as well.

The principle of self-determination is, obviously the most important ideological principle of the "Realists." This principle, though underlying everything they write and say, is not, however frequently spelled out and discussed in their publications. The ideology of those native "Realists" is oriented towards activism rather than philosophy. They are modern activists, well aware of time limitations, the impact of mass media and the existence of strategic moments and strategic audiences. They know where, when and to whom to present their demands, and they know how to present them. During one of the important congresses for instance which took place in 1973, they were given only three minutes to speak and they managed to condense their key-demands into the following three points:

1. Indian leaders should be consulted on matters concerning all Indian affairs.
2. Government should combat economic exploitation of Indians by enforcing the sale of their products at the prices of the market, not—as has been the case—below market prices.
3. Indians at all levels should be representing themselves without non-Indian intermediaries.

I asked my interviewees many "embarrassing" questions which neither puzzled nor embarrassed them. I asked one of them for instance whether they had ever thought of creating a truly Indian nation in Mexico. "Oh, no"—he said, smiling bitterly—"we do not have any suicidal tendencies whatsoever." I asked him then whether they ever advocated the Indianization of Mexico instead of Mexicanization of Indians. "This is just impossible," he answered, "there is, as you know, no one single Indian culture in Mexico but many of them. Which of those cultures, which Indian language should we select to Indianize Mexico? No, this is simply impossible . . . and we *are* realists . . ." To probe further into their vision of the future, I provocatively suggested that with the integration of Indians into national society traditional Indian village governments would certainly disappear. "Why should they disappear with the integration of Indians!" exclaimed my interviewee. "I think they will never disappear!" I did not ask him to explain how the integration of Indians could possibly be combined with the preservation of their traditional Indian governments. I did not ask any more questions on this topic because I do understand only too well that whatever our rational, realistic programs may be, there are certain implications of those programs, certain perspectives, which we cannot simply emotionally accept . . . about which we cannot rationally converse at least for some time.

Besides the principle of self-determination, the principle of social justice, understood in a strictly secular and contemporary manner, seems to be equally important. "The only effective help which the Indian needs is the prompt application of democracy and social justice" we read in an editorial in *Cuadernos del AMPII* of June 1968, and this statement seems to be quite characteristic of their thinking.

"We want to do for Indians what Hidalgo and other heroes of Mexican Independence did for others" one of the interviewees told me. "We want education and social justice for our people. Everyone should have a mastery of the national language, and the standard of living promised by the Mexican Revolution . . ."

Such tasks are considered extremely urgent. Writing on behalf of such causes and exposing the deviations from the ideals of Mexican Revolution has been customary in the *Cuadernos del AMPII* and in the special pamphlets published on various occasions. Such instant-commentaries are merged with instant and continuous lobbying activities. "Realists" try to be everywhere that the Indian situation may be discussed, and during the current decade it has been discussed in connection with all major national problems. They try to attend all important congresses and conferences, without interrupting, however, their intensive work on the community level. According to an article, for instance, in *Cuadernos del AMPII* (No. 1, 1967) intellectuals from AMPII gave professional orientation and economic help to more than four hundred local Committees of Development and Improvement (*Comites de Mejoramiento y Desarrollo*). "To educate people in such a way that they would understand their immediate local conditions is one of our most important objectives," one of the "Realists" assured me, "But do not think," he added, "that I have in mind the development of a democratic social consciousness among them. Indian masses are not yet ready for this, neither are they ready for democratic political consciousness. We have to be much more modest. We have been trying to educate people to see their local conditions realistically: to understand what they could do themselves and what they should and have the right to ask for. They are confused about such matters. We have been trying to tell them also that not everything one tries to achieve is always achieved. We have been trying to give them a realistic approach to their problems, and to inspire them with moral courage. . . . This is essential . . ."

Their past is seen as marked by irreparable defeat (Spanish invasion of their lands) and by centuries of oppression, illuminated by very short periods of betterment and hope. Those short periods (Independence; the presidency of the Zapotec native, Benito Juarez; the Mexican Revolution of 1910; the presidency of Lázaro Cárdenas, and recently the presidency of Luis Echaverriá) are seen as results of the efforts of exceptional men, idealistic and seriously concerned with social justice rather than specifically with Indian fate. Even Benito Juarez, the greatest hero of my interviewees, is seen by them as acting on behalf of all unjustly treated, not specifically on behalf of Indians.

Apart from those exceptional men the Indianist policies of Independent Mexico are regarded by them as a modified continuation of colonial policies. "They do not try to exterminate us physically today but they try to exterminate our culture. This is the future," one of the

"Realists" told me. "Yes, our future is cultural extermination . . . "

But this gloomy realism does not paralyze their activities. Quite the contrary . . . it seems to stimulate their efforts to find a place for Indians within this inevitably non-Indian Mexican reality, to find this place as painlessly and as peacefully as possible.

Their individual moral dilemmas are, no doubt, complicated and difficult but the objectives of their movement are clear and simple. The ideology of this movement is revisionistic, minimalistic, populist, secular and politically active. The political and social structure of Mexico is taken for granted and only slight modifications of this structure are proposed. The movement promotes social justice for the Indian masses as the most unjustly treated segment of Mexican society. It struggles to achieve this justice in a minimalistic rather than maximalistic manner, even if only a partial justice, but as soon as possible. Though many of the "Realists" expressed doubts whether the full equality of opportunity and treatment will be achieved for Indians during their lifetime, they did not do any planning for the future generations. Their ideology has been designed for one generation only, and so have their strategies. If they do not succeed as well as they would like to succeed, future "Realists" will know better than they do how to act in their times. Some of the younger "Realists" experiment with new approaches within or on the margins of the movement. They do not justify anything either in terms of such metaphysical entities as "History" or "Revolution" or in terms of "Destiny" . . . They do not promise salvation or happiness in the other world, and unlike many nativist movements they do not rely on any "revelations." Their ideology stresses immediate strategies rather than philosophical, metaphysical or theological principles. It urges firm commitments to the key objectives of the Movement but it advises flexibility of strategies for achievement of its unflexible, though minimalistic goals. In terms of its scope it is an ethnic ideology: segmental rather than universalistic. In fact we may say that the "Realists" have been trying to transform Mexican Indians into ethnic groups within the culturally pluralistic rather than monocultural Mexican society. They have not tried (in spite of their emphasis on social justice and equality) to relate the fate of Indians to the fate of other underprivileged rural and urban non-Indian groups. The universalistic ideological themes, such as equality and justice, are seen by them mainly in the context of contemporary Mexican Indian human condition—not in terms of mankind, native America or even total Mexican society.

7. Their Identities

Unlike the village natives from the state of Chiapas[10] and Central Mexico[11] who referred to themselves always as Tzeltales and Mazahuas, never as "Indians," the "Realists" insist on calling themselves "Indians." This is how the member of this movement is supposed to identify himself publicly, whatever the private pitfalls of his identification. Tzeltales from Chiapas, more isolated and traditionalistic than Mazahuas, insist on being called "Tzeltales" since this is their old tribal identity. "That is what we are," they say. They may be called, and sometimes they refer to themselves as, *gente de aquí* (people from here) or as *gente humilde* (simple folk) but never as "Indians" since the term "Indian" is used either in a derogatory or, at best, patronizing manner in this area. Mazahuas whom I studied knew that the term "Indian" was imposed on them by the Spaniards, and this has been their additional reason for rejecting it. They too identify themselves as "people from here" or "simple folk," insisting however, on being called "Mazahuas" whenever in contact with strangers.

The professionals from AMPII insist on their realism. They see Mexican natives as reduced by Spanish invaders to being "Indians." They were conquered, humiliated, deprived of their tribal identities, exploited, discriminated against, and this condition, though modified by several short periods of betterment, still generally persists among the native masses in Mexico. As long as those native populations are not integrated into the national society, the educated Zapotecs, Nahuas, Mixtecs, Purépechas, Popolocos, Otomies will insist on calling themselves "Indians," whatever the degree of their own personal integration into Mexican national society, whatever their fluency in Spanish, whatever their professional successes. "As soon as we achieve social justice for the Indian masses," one of my interviewees told me, "I will identify as Indian only on a folkloric level. You see well yourself that I am really Mexican . . . " This may seem like a contradictory statement if understood literally. In fact, however, it means a strong emphasis on alternatives and choice. Responsibility for those with whom one grew up under difficult circumstances, and who are still facing enormous difficulties, was chosen here as the most important value by my informant.

More extreme cases of similar choices could be observed among some of the often completely Polonized, Germanized or Hollandized Jews of nazi-invaded Europe. Some of these Poles, Germans, and Dutchmen of even quite remote Jewish ancestry chose to identify as Jews at the time of the greatest nazi persecution; some of them even went voluntarily to the ghettos to face death together with "their own people" whose language they had often ignored and whose culture and religion was foreign to them.

During times of religious persecutions some atheists return as well to their former religions, if not as believers, at least as sympathizers. The mythology of the past, however supressed, must be, indeed, very strong among defeated human groups, in order to revive in some of their people, such a sense of responsibility, such courage and heroism.

Identity means above all commitment, commitment of scarce resources (time, money, health) to whatever we consider to be most important. Though identity is an attitude tested above all through action, in modern, complex societies there is nothing simple about such action, and nothing stable about our identities. Unlike our preindustrial ancestors, faced with relatively few choices, we have to choose constantly and each such new choice may force us to revive our old identities.

All "Realists" were born and raised in Indian villages where they acquired more or less firm identifications with their respective Indian groups. Some acquired pride in their past and a great respect for their ancestors; some only learned to respect the tremendous efforts of their contemporaries, especially their own parents, efforts necessary to survive and to preserve their dignity in the midst of a predatory world. All of them learned during those years that to be Zapotec, Nahua, Otomie is not an easy fate, and all learned about a difficult alternative, that of becoming a Mexican detached from one's origin. Some of their friends and relatives chose this difficult path. Coming out of a variety of cultures and a variety of social situations, they all had in their late childhood quite similar views of the future. This future was ambiguous and threatening. To remain Zapotec, Nahua, Otomie within the world with no prospect for the continuous existence and development of Zapotec, Nahua, Otomie communities, was not an easy choice, indeed. Their parents sometimes advised them "to better themselves" and tried to give them courage to "go into the world." Some of the parents hesitated, however: in some periods they wanted them to "go into the world," in others they would discourage them, pointing out the hardships ahead. Contacts with those from the larger world: teachers, merchants, relatives returning from work in the cities . . . all those influences shaped their childhood and pressed them to make a difficult choice. As I described, all the interviewed "Realists" chose to leave their villages and most of them graduated from the Indian *internados*. In those schools their identifications were shaped, identifications as Mexican citizens with the full right and duty of national participation but with equally strong responsibility toward "those left behind." After acquiring their education they were to return to their villages as community leaders but most of them did not return. They took their initiation into Mexican national ideology seriously, drew logical conclusions out of what they learned, and decided to go to the capital instead of returning to their villages since only from the center of the power—they reasoned—would they be able to influence their villages' conditions.

During the difficult university years this type of identification was strongly maintained through their youth organization, *Confederación de Jovenes Indígenas* (Confederation of Indian Youth) and later through AMPII (Association of Mexican Indian Professionals and Intellectuals).

From my interviews with the "Realists" emerges an interesting picture of their social movement. This social movement has a srong and stable ideology, continuous inspiring democratically oriented leadership, a rather loose social structure (relatively few strongly enforced norms) and a curiously floating membership.

PART II: UTOPIANS

UTOPIANS YESTERDAY

1. In Their Own Societies

Several great civilizations—Maya, Nahua, (and later Aztec), Zapotec and Mixtec—flourished within the boundaries of today's Mexico and fragments of their architecture, works of art and writings have survived until today. Some descendants of those civilizations have never become reconciled to the European invasion and have been cultivating their language and traditions throughout the centuries with impressive courage, faith and determination.

Though archeological findings, still incomplete, have been throwing more and more light on the culture and even some aspects of the social structure of those great civilizations, very little, so far, can be inferred from those data about the social roles of the makers of those civilizations. We know close to nothing about Zapotec, Mixtec and even Maya[1] intellectuals.[2] We know a little more about Nahua elites since their enormous state, (known variously as the "Confederation of Anauk," "Anauac," "Aztec Empire") was in full flower at the time of the Spanish invasion.[3] Though the Spaniards destroyed almost all works of architecture, art and literature of the invaded people, they left nevertheless admiring descriptions of the greatness of their material culture and some accounts of their customs, which in spite of inaccuracies and biases still serve as important sources for contemporary americanist scholars throughout the world.[4] As soon as the invasion was more or less completed, Spaniards began to teach the Latin alphabet and Spanish language to selected descendants of the native nobility, mainly Aztecs, and made them write first-hand accounts of their customs, beliefs, contemporary historical events, and to reconstruct as much as possible of their science and literature. No doubt, this reconstruction of Nahuatl culture was motivated mostly by the desire of the Spaniards to understand-in-order-to-control but this was, certainly, not the only motivation. Though not from the highest strata of Spanish society, the Spanish invaders or at least their decision-making elites, were men from Renaissance Europe whose admiration for cultural refinements was certainly as great as that of even the poorest Americans from the era of early capitalism for the Wall Street financial glories. Besides, there was something to gain by sending back to Spain accounts of destroyed treasures "which were produced with the help of demons" by those "conquered pagans" who were now to be "saved, reeducated and incorporated into the Christian Empire."

Since in order to cultivate arts, literature and reflection, one has to have some minimum leisure, the precolonial American intellectuals of this area did not have to till their own land. They were all of the upper and ruling classes, and their power, social commitment and prestige within their respective populations were enormous. The phenomenon of monastic intellectualism, such as existed in the same periods in Asia and Europe, was unknown in this area. Though often isolated from others through their semi-divine status, those native American intellectuals, however critical of their own society or society in general[5] were never alienated from their societies, as are so many outstanding occidental intellectuals today.

According to the accounts of Aztec noblemen educated in the earliest colonial colleges of Tapepulco and Tlatelolco, the Nahua intellectual, *tlamatini*, was supposed not only to be "a light, a torch which does not smoke" but he was also to apply "his light to the world," to "direct people and things, to guide human affairs."[6] They were frankly elitists: they assumed a patronizing and protective responsibility toward the masses, taking for granted their own right to superior education, their high prestige, their decision-making capacities. All of them were very likely major or minor public figures, leaders of their respective peoples. We know that occasionally they questioned and even rejected some aspects of their own culture; those were however, most likely the engaged, insiders' critiques and rejections.

There were no detached critics-outsiders among precolonial intellectuals of this area, and there were no remote, monk-like intellectuals either since priests were always members of the ruling class and rulers performed some priestly functions.

2. Spanish Invasion

Though the Spanish invasion affected, naturally, all groups of the invaded territory, it will be treated in this chapter mainly as a confrontation between the Aztec elite and the Spanish invaders. Aristocratic Aztec sages were all committed leaders, priests and warriors of their expanding state. They all accepted the hierarchical character of their society, obeyed their deities or their superiors, assumed leadership over inferiors, and were convinced of their ecological, life-preserving, and civilizing mission. This mission was rooted in their sacred cosmology, which for them was like science for nineteenth century Europeans. Their daily life alternated between administrative duties, religious and literary feasts and warfare. Their future was clouded by a variety of vague and often contradictory predictions and prophecies. Their long-deceased divine ruler, Quetzalcoatl, was to come back to assume leadership but at the same time there existed a possibility of the great decline, of the very end of their epoch—and of the world.

When the ambassadors of Cortés arrived at the court of the Aztec ruler in Tenochtitlan, Emperor Montezuma assumed at first they were coming to him from Quetzalcoatl. But since they were poorly dressed, exhausted, confused, hungry, and did not behave in any sense like the envoys of a divine ruler, Montezuma and his advisors became suspicious, and did not receive them. The word accompanied by luxurious gifts was sent to Cortés that Montezuma would gladly accept him personally but would not negotiate with those commoners who claimed to be his ambassadors. In response to his message Cortés announced his personal arrival in Tenochtitlan. But by the time this announcement reached Tenochtitlan, Montezuma, through various reports on the behavior of the invaders, through further interpretation of ancient prophecies, through frightening dreams about the coming destruction of Tenochtitlan, became even more hesitant about this strange man who, maybe was, but maybe was not the expected Quetzalcoatl. He found a compromise solution to this bewildering situation, and sent another message to Cortés asking him to wait until his death before taking over the leadership of Anauak. This advice must have been very surprising to Cortés who knew nothing about the Quetzalcoatl legend. At once he started a careful slow march on Tenochtitlan, learning as much as possible during this journey in order to be ready for the successful seizure of power. During this long journey he made pacts with those groups who were dissatisfied with the Aztec rule, and promised them liberation. At the same time he kept cultivating and promulgating for the authorities of the Confederation the image of an important and benevolent visitor, whose arrival was somehow related to the future of Anauak . . .[7]

There are many versions of the dramatic encounter between Montezuma and Cortés in Tenochtitlan, and many irresponsible speculations about what was going on in the mind of the Aztec ruler before and during this confrontation. Whatever happened, however, at the time of this encounter, whether Montezuma "weakened" and surrendered his power to Cortés, or whether he was tricked by him into some sort of compromise, we may be reasonably sure about the following consequences of this meeting:

1. Montezuma and a number of his high advisors were taken prisoner and later murdered by the invaders.
2. Tenochtitlan was plundered by the victorious Spanish army helped by a number of native allies.
3. The main temple of Aztec god, Huitzilopochtli, was destroyed and many people (among them a great number of Aztec elites) were massacred.
4. The population of Tenochtitlan (and probably of the immediate area as well) became sharply polarized. Some continued as well as they could their armed resistance; others were more passive, and we do not know what the motives for this passivity were. Possibly this category was further subdivided into (a) those who plotted more careful future resistance, consulting their gods and elders, (b) those who dedicated themselves to rescuing whatever could be rescued from the sacred and secular treasures of Anauak, and (c) those who were making the first steps toward collaboration with the invadors.

We know that after the occupation of the capital there were various rebellions within the city, and that Cortés had to escape from Tenochtitlan with his army. We also know that with a reconstructed army Cortés returned to Tenochtitlan, and then, under a new ruler, Cuitlahuac, and after his death under the leadership of his young nephew, Cuahtémoc, the famous three-months battle for Tenochtitlan took place. In this battle most of the city was destroyed and about 240,000 people of its 300,000 population, were killed (among them almost all the Aztec aristocracy).[8] We also know that in the early morning, August 13, 1521, Cauhtémoc was taken prisoner in the canals of the adjacent town of Tlatelolco. We know that before he was captured (in the night of August 12-13), those who survived from Anauak's Great Council, *Ueyi Tlahtohkan*, had issued a manifesto in which the coming defeat was announced, and the instructions were given on how the population of the defeated state should behave during the forthcoming occupation, while awaiting the moment in which "the sun rises again."

UTOPIANS TODAY

1. Origins, Silhouettes, Images

In the mid-1940s, a group of young Mexican professionals from Mexico City founded a Movement of Reappearance of Anauak designed to help "the sun rise again" not only for Mexico but, eventually, for the whole Amercan continent as well. These young men and women were just starting out in their respective professions. It is possible that in this atmosphere of accidental, unplanned, economic growth tightening contacts with U. S. investors, and rapid Americanization under the impact of the mass media,[1] these young Mexican intellectuals, still taking very seriously the pro-native themes of Mexican Revolution, better travelled, more affluent and better read than others, were stimulated to start "something new"; to "revive," to "awake," and to find a place for themselves within this booming country heading into an unknown direction.

Since I did not interview this Movement's members I can only reconstruct their social origins on the basis of my own observations during several social gatherings (combined with my relatively good knowledge of various strata of Mexican society[2]), and on the basis of what those "Utopians" write about themselves in their magazine *Izkalotl*. What I heard about them from various outsiders to the Movement and what I read occasionally in the national press was also helpful in those reconstructions.

Most of them, for instance, seem to be of urban origin, relatively well-to-do and well-connected. Many of them were probably born in professional or middle class business families, partially of native origins (as most Mexicans are) but certainly not of "pure Indian blood". Such social origins are underplayed however, and even disguised in their ideological writings, similar to the way the middle class or aristocratic origins are downplayed by the numerous European leaders of socialist parties. "Utopians" stress their rural Nahua origins and connections strongly, though most of them, very likely, were born in Mexico City and learned Nahuatl (in most cases only some Nahuatl) mainly through their involvement in the Movement.

All Utopian movements, as all great religions, should be seen as complex multidimensional structures. Their language, for instance, may be on some occasions matter of fact, on other occasions highly metaphorical or ritualistic, their institutions may be both secular and religious, and the motivations of their members on some occasions practical and even "materialistic," on other occasions "idealistic" and mystical. Without an understanding of such complexities, we are bound to misunderstand the "Utopians," to see them as contradicting themselves, as being phony, hypocrytical or deceitful.

It is very easy to impute and extremely hard to judge fairly the motivations of those involved in contemporary social movements even if we study them more directly than I studied the "Utopians." Do they really care about the people for whom the movement is designed or are they merely dedicated to their own self-realization, or alleviation of guilt feelings? Do they really believe in their ideology, their mission, their legitimacy? Or do they use this only to manipulate their followers? Such questions and many others were asked, probably about leaders of all movements by their contemporaries. We have to wait, sometimes for decades or centuries, to get the whole picture of a given movement, to understand its impact upon society and to judge the moral worth of its leaders.

Despite the mysterious, metaphorical language which they use in their sacred writings (published usually in separate columns side by side with secular writings) in their magazine *Izkalotl*, despite the "loud silence" of their well-researched neo-Aztec ceremonies, the members of this Movement look,[3] behave and probably live their daily lives like any other middle and upper-middle class Mexicans. They have a typical Mexican way of speaking with generous outgoing gestures, so in contrast to the restraint and calmness characteristic of contemporary Mexican Indians and so in contrast with their own ceremonial behavior. Nor does this secular political rhetoric differ much from the patriotic revolutionary rhetoric of typical Mexican politicians.

The men of the Movement dress formally while in the city, as do all other Mexican professionals, but they wear sport outfits, modest but carefully chosen and definitely casual, during their country outings. Women have their hair done in a formal way: usually they have permanents and sometimes their hair is tinted red or blonde. Gathering all my courage I asked one of the Movement's women why "being Aztec" she did not wear an Indian hair-style. Not in the least embarrassed by my question she answered that at home she had a very nice wig made out of her own long, straight dark hair which she used for ceremonies. This was her Aztec hair-do, but in her daily life (she was a school-inspector) this permanented hair was much more comfortable.

Like other Mexican women, the women of the Movement wear high heels and rather elaborate and stylish fitted dresses. Their abundant jewelry is sometimes of native type, and, as they emphasize, "always inspired by Aztec motifs." During country outings and on special occasions they often wear contemporary native garmets so popular with tourists but more carefully chosen, and often authentic. They wear them very proudly and consciously and they are well informed about each item's exact origin.

They dress their children in a similar manner, and though all the Movement's members mainly speak Spanish among themselves, they often call their children by their Movement-acquired Aztec first names. Adults use those Aztec names more rarely and more self-consciously among themselves.

Their Movement is apparently sponsored only by their own contributions, which is emphasized over and over again in the Movement's monthly magazine *Izkalotl*. But they seem to lack neither money nor generosity as becomes obvious when one reads descriptions of the numerous gatherings, "magnificient suppers", outings and ceremonies, described in *Izkalotl*. Some of the richer members themselves sponsor such events.

All of them claim to be "Nahuas," or "Aztecs" and many insist on their "close connection with rural Nahuatl speakers." Though some say they are of "pure Nahua blood, descendants of ancient Aztecs," they never try to pass for those "simple, pure, rural Nahuas" whom they idolize in their publications, as carriers of the ancient tradition. Unlike populist ideologists they do not apologize for their higher education, upper middle class status and connections. The members of this movement (though deeply concerned with political mobilization of native masses) are as frankly elitist, as were their Aztec "forefathers."

Most "Utopians" work in such prestigious positions as lawyers, professors, doctors, engineers, teachers, writers; some are financially well-off and have travelled extensively in Europe and the Americas. They are well-connected in metropolitan Mexican society, attend important congresses and meetings, hold public office, and a few of them are quite well-known in Mexico.

The membership of such prominent Mexican professionals in the Movement of Reappearance of Anauk is either unknown in the larger society or considered only one of the minor aspects of their full lives. Writing for *Izkalotl* (the official organ of the movement, appearing regularly every month; the name, *Izkalotl*, means in Nahuatl "Reappearance"), speaking Nahuatl, participation in Nahua ceremonies by those professionals, is considered by their Mexican peers a purely cultural (and definitely not political) activity, a nostalgically attractive activity since the strong emphasis on native origins, so central to post-revolutionary times, has been lost for some time in Mexico. The revival of this emphasis by intellectuals from *Izkalotl* is therefore most welcome among the somewhat stifled but still vaguely restless middle-age "revolutionary" intellectuals. Even the Party of Mexicanity which was born out of the Movement a few years before the death of its founder and leader, Rodolfo Nieva, has been accepted by the Mexican "revolutionary" intellectuals as a cultural rather than political party, in spite of its clearly political platform. Many friends of the leader sent their contributions, and in a few cases only (as evidenced by the letters to the editor of *Izkalotl*) did they become alarmed with the ideas of this group (such as, for instance, the proposed rejection of Spanish as a national language), and withdraw their unqualified endorsement. But this withdrawal was done rather quietly (without publicity in the national press) and *Izkalotl* did not make a great issue out of those few rejections either.

Among the "Realists" whom I interviewed, only some seemed to know vaguely about the Movement of Reappearance of Anauak. None of them knew about their magazine *Izkalotl*, and no one was informed about the Movement's structure and its activities. Some of them spoke of "various groups of Nahuatl speaking natives, dancing in their native costumes on the ruins of their ancient temples"[4]; others condemned "those Nahuas" for being just "another political platform, using poor natives for gaining political power." Some accused them of being "elitists" and "racists," who claim that Aztecs had higher civilizations than Zapotecs, Mixtecs and even Mayas, and insist on their own superiority on those grounds. Others referred to the Movement as an "underground Nahua government" hinting vaguely and hesitantly that there was, maybe, some continuity between the ancient Aztecs and the leaders of the Movement.

2. Life Cycle of the Movement

At the time of my research the Movement of Reappearance of Anauak was about twenty-five years old, and, obviously, less dynamic and less optimistic than during the first decade of its activities. "Ingeniero X," my first contact with the Movement, and as it soon appeared one of the Movement's leaders was at that time between fifty-five and sixty years old, while the other members of the Movement whom I met during several Movement-sponsored lectures and ceremonies ranged from their early twenties to late sixties, with the core members however more or less the age of "Ingeniero X." Unlike the "Realists," there were many women among the "Utopians" whom I met on several occasions and many children, initiated from birth into the Movement's culture. Family units, it seems, participated in the Movement, sometimes quite large families, including nieces, nephews and their children.

Though respectful of its second leader, the Movement at the time of my research had not yet fully recovered from the death in 1969 of its beloved founder. Photographs of licenciado Rodolfo Nieva were reproduced, and his words were quoted in numerous articles in *Izkalotl.* Members of the Movement spoke of him with the greatest reverence and with tears in their eyes. His multiple titles, both sacred and secular, his functions and merits, have been publicized in all the Movement's publications:

> He was a graduate in Law of National University in Mexico (UNAM).
> He was President of the Mexican Bar Association.
> He was a member of the International Association of Lawyers.
> He was creator of the doctrine of Mexicanity (*Mexikayotl* in Nahuatl).
> He was *Ue Tekuhtli del Ollin Kalpultin Teizkaliliztli* (literally: Great Master of Authority of the Highest Governmental Council of the Confederated Movement of the Reappearance of Anauak).
> He was as well *Ue Tekuhtli Nauatlahtolkalli anozo Mexikatlahtolkalli* (Great Master of Authority in the Academy of Nahuatl language).
> And he was also *Tlayekanki Tlaxelol Mexicayotl Anauaka Nemilil Nechikolli* (Director of the Academy of Nahuatl Philosophy of the Institute of the Culture of Anauak).[5]

In *Izkalotl* of March 1970, we find an article called "The Stages of Life of Rodolfo Nieva". We learn from this article something about those moments of Rodolfo Nieva's life which probably inspired and prepared him to start the Movement of Reappearance of Anauak.

During his university years (in law school), Rodolfo Nieva founded a National League of Students from which emerged the Nationalistic Students' Party. On the ticket of this party he ran for the office of *regidor* in one of the districts of Mexico City. He won and soon afterwards became the *Presidente Municipal* of this particular district. Later, we learn, Rodolfo Nieva, as an established lawyer, was among the founders of the Mexican Bar Association. We also read in this article and many others, published in *Izkalotl* after his death in 1969, about his various travels, attendances at national and international congresses and his important contacts.

Deeply rooted in Mexican society, highly respected by his peers, more modest, probably, and more persistent than most of them, Rodolfo Nieva had perfect qualifications to create a movement which would be not only tolerated but eventually accepted by the Mexican power elites. He appealed to them in terms of the Mexican Revolution, economic development and the elimination of corruption from public life; familiar and respectable appeals, presented, however, with more emphasis on the neglected native heritage and on the prominent place of Mexico within the family of modern nations.

With this background Rodolfo Nieva was certainly well-prepared for the task of organizing the Party of Mexicanity (*Partido de Mexicanidad*) which was in the future to enter presidential elections, and, after its eventual victory, to implement in Mexico a large-scale revisionistic program.

We may wonder in fact whether Rodolfo Nieva was equally well-prepared for his primary task: the formation of the semi-secret Movement of the Reappearance of Anauak of which the Party of Mexicanity was the secular organ. We ask ourselves how such a practical, efficient and busy modern lawyer could have formulated the Movement's sacred ideology. Reading *Izkalotl* we find that even as a young man Rodolfo Nieva was devoted to Nahua scholarship and that he cultivated this involvement throughout his life in spite of his other absorbing professional and political activities. We learn also that he was helped in his scholarly pursuits and rewriting of Nahua History by other key scholars of the Movement such as Ignacio Romerovargas[6], Juan Luna Cárdenas[7], and the Movement's endorsed controversial Mexican anthropologist Eulalia Guzman[8] as well as by his own sister María del Carmen Nieva Lopez.[9]

The life history of the Movement of Reappearance of Anauak may be roughly divided into four periods:

1. The period from the formation of the Movement in the late 1940s till the publication of the first issue of the Movement's monthly *Izkalotl* in 1960.
2. The years from the publication of the first issue of *Izkalotl* in 1960 till the formation of the Party of Mexicanity (*Partido de Mexicanidad*) in 1965.
3. The period from the formation of the Party of Mexicanity (1965) till the death of the Movement's founder in 1969.
4. The years from the death of the Movement's founder (1969) till the present.

It seems that the most dynamic periods of the Movement were those just before the appearance of *Izkalotl* and after, until the Party of Mexicanity became organized. Those two periods correspond also to the most energetic years of the Movement's still young but already well-established leaders.

During the first period most of the numerous units and sub-units were organized, and during this period its style of action became well established as well.

It is essential to understand the dual, bi-cultural, Mexican-Nahua style in order to understand the development of this complex nativistic movement.

This bi-cultural style can be best clarified by briefly describing the three distinct publics to which the Movement tries to appeal through its various activities:

First of all it tries to appeal to Mexican national society and particularly to its power elites.

Being registered with an appropriate national office as a voluntary organization of a cultural character, the Movement tries to present to the Mexican nation an image of a voluntary association devoted to archeological, linguistic, historical and anthropological research into Nahua culture, and to legitimize its activities in terms of pro-native ideals of Mexican Revolution. The type of discourse used in such Mexican-nation-directed speeches and publications does not differ much from political discourse current in other Mexican social movements. Secularity, humanism, native, but particularly Aztec, heritage, adherence to the ideals of the Mexican Rvolution, are stressed with a similar type of exaltation as they are stressed in all other Mexican speeches and manifestos. The revival of some native customs, and even the ceremonial use of Nahuatl language,[10] have been for a long time a part of Mexican political folklore, so this emphasis does not look peculiar.

The party of Mexicanity which emerged from the Movement in 1965 in order eventually to enter the presidential elections, was organized along the same lines as other Mexican political parties, many of which also failed to be recognized by the government "for lack of formal qualifications." This party is vaguely known in Mexico as a "small, highly intellectual, native heritage-emphasizing party, neither left nor right-wing, and rather friendly to PRI, the party in power."

Second, the Movement tries to appeal to "the larger world."

International relations of the Movement are carried out with the help of similar images and similar types of discourse. Members of various embassies, consulates, and other foreign groups are invited to "spectacular suppers," organized by the Movement in the most elegant restaurants and clubs of the capital. During these events the members of the Movement appear usually in their well-researched precolonial Aztec garments, address themselves by their newly acquired Aztec names, and show to the enchanted foreigners carefully staged and slightly reinterpreted ancient Aztec ceremonial dances. Those events are always described in *Izkalotl*, and the names of the distinguished guests are enumerated.

Such performances are, probably, received by the guests in a mood similar to one in which they receive the famous Mexican Folkloric Ballet, so popular with foreigners. It is possible, however, that during such feasts some lobbying on behalf of the "real purpose" of the Movement is being done among the better known and sympathetic guests. The members of the Movement of the Reappearance of Anauak claim to have their "ambassadors" in many foreign countries, "from New York to Peru," some of them, apparently, Nahuas or part-Nahuas, some sympathetic foreigners. Reference to those ambassadors can be found occasionally in *Izakalotl*.

Finally, the Movement tries to appeal to "their own people."

They address themselves in a different way to "their own people" who consist of "two branches—one is that of pure Mexicans" to quote from the textbook of Nahuatl language published by the Movement,[11] "the other is made of mixed-Mexicans, who have been living within Hispanic-European culture, speak Spanish and keep our country dominated by that culture."

"Pure Mexicans," that is, "Pure Nahuas," are glorified in *Izkalotl* as the carriers of old Aztec traditions from which all others could learn a great deal. Pilgrimages are made by the Movement's leaders to those old Nahuas living in the isolated places in the mountains. An air of mystery and reverance can be found in all writing on such people in *Izkalotl*.

For "mixed-Mexicans" (partially Nahua), potential recruits to the Movement, a special column is devoted in *Izkalotl*. They are actively recruited into the Movement, accused of keeping their country under foreign domination, informed about the "true History" of their fatherland, "Great Anauak," and about what they should do in order to contribute to her full reappearance and reconstruction.

At the end of the second, and throughout the third, stage of the Movement's development, the emphasis shifted, it seems, from the building of ideology, organizations and active recruitment (all involving an air of sacredness) to more secular political activities centered around the building of the Party of Mexicanity and complementary propagandistic and diplomatic activities.

The Party failed to meet legal requirements to be an officially recognized political party, eligible to enter presidential elections. This failure, which must have affected greatly the Movement's members, was followed by a much greater catastrophe in the death of their admired founder, Rodolfo Nieva. Though a new leader was elected according to "appropriate ancient Aztec procedures" of "the most perfect democracy" (as members of the Movement like to emphasize), the Movement was definitely shaken, weakened and changed by this unexpected "return to nature" of its so highly respected founder.

The Party of Mexicanity "went to sleep and was waiting for an appropriate moment to start a new fight for legal recognition," as "ingeniero X" put it, and the emphasis of the Movement shifted again from strongly secular and political activity to the more mystical. A myth surrounding the deceased founder occupies much place in *Izkalotl*, and more attention, it seems, is now given to the recruitment, re-Nahuaisation, and organization of suburban rural Nahuas who had forgotten much of their Nahua culture but did not, apparently, lose their identification.

3. The New History

If we define scholarly history as a careful objective description of the past, there exist, indeed, very few such histories. Most histories are either iconoclastic or mythological or both iconoclastic and mythological. Iconoclastic histories challenge, ridicule or destroy those interpretations of the past which they consider incorrect and damaging for the group to which they belong or with which they sympathize. Mythological histories elaborate, endorse, and glorify such interpretations of the past which are acceptable, morale-building, considered useful or even indispensable for the functioning of a given group.

The history elaborated by the Movement of Reappearance of Anauak is of a mixed, iconoclastic-mythological character. It challenges official Mexican history and it elaborates and promotes the new "true History."

"Our New History started only in 1957," we read in the first issue of *Izkalotl* (September 1968). "It started with the writings of Romerovargas and Eulalia Guzmán." Those two prominent and controversial scholars on the basis of their archeological and historical research have challenged a great deal of precolonial and colonial history. "Pre-Cauhtémoc history (history from before the execution of Cauhtémoc, the last Aztec ruler), as taught today is full of falsities" we read in *Izkalotl* of October, 1960. "It is based on chronicles written by Spaniards to justify invasion. The narrowness of fanatic religious criteria prevented the Spaniards from understanding a culture much superior to their own."

Some of those challenges have been recognized by Mexican archeologists and historians, some not, and polemics are still alive. The "true History" endorsed by the Movement is, naturally, greatly simplified, as all official histories with a capital "H" are.[12] The history of Anauak, as presented here, is a popular history, such as may be taught to those converts to the Movement who did not have the chance to acquire higher education, and to the first generation of children brought up within the Movement.

According to the prehistory of Anauak briefly presented in the November 1964 issue of *Izkalotl*, in an article entitled "Atlantida," we read that

> "Atlantida was our Anauak, and its inhabitants *Atlantes* were Nahuas, our ancestors from the era of Teotihuacan. The name of the Atlantic Ocean is a Nahuatl name. Plato compiled his data about Atlantida (the legend well-known in Europe) from the information which Solon, the Greek sage, brought home from Egypt.
> Fantastic people arrived in Egypt, the carriers of magnificent culture. These people kept repeating the word "Atlantika," which in Nahuatl means 'we arrived through water.'

The Egyptians called them 'Atlantees' and gave the name 'Atlantida' to the land from which they came. The Egyptians started looking for Atlantida along the coasts of the ocean which they called 'Atlantic,' and this is how the legend was born, the legend of Atlantida governed by a woman.

But the truth is different: during the era of Teotihuacan one of the groups of Nahuas was led by a woman and for this reason a split within the country was threatened. In order to avoid such a conflict, she decided to emigrate through the sea and this is how she and her followers were lost in the Atlantic, crossed to Gibraltar and landed in Egypt. In this way, Nahuas, known as 'Atlantes,' brought to Egypt the idea of pyramids and many other concepts, such as for instance the concept of God, *Teo*, which the Greeks transformed into Deo.[13]

The article ends with the following prediction: "In the same way as the Nahuatl culture influenced Egyptian and Greek cultures, the culture of our reconstructed fatherland, Anauak, will influence other foreign cultures."

Much space in *Izkalotl* is devoted to the idea that Anauak was not an empire, but a confederation, the name "empire" being introduced by Spaniards who thought ethnocentrically in terms of their own concepts. In the October, 1967 issue of *Izkalotl* there is an historical article by Rodolfo Nieva, the leader of the Movement:

Anauak was never an 'Aztec Empire' but a Confederation of Sovereign States governed by Mexico-Tenochtitlan, Texcoco, and Tlalcopan, governed democratically by the elected governors at a time when Europe completely lacked democracy since she had hereditary, absolute, arbitrary monarchs.

We read in August 1961 issue of *Izkalotl*:

Aztecs, (one of the seven Nahua groups) never governed in Anauak. In accordance with the Destiny of our Race, as soon as they arrived in the valley of Mexico, they founded the City of Mexico-Tenochtitlan and created the country of Mexicatl, that is of Mexican people, in order to carry on the already mentioned Destiny. Soon afterwards, satisfied with their accomplished mission, they disappeared.

We learn from the same article that the "territory of Anauak extended from the Mexican lands now under United States occupation to Nicaragua," and in various other articles and columns in *Izkalotl* the theme of the establishment of such an enormous Confederation "through peaceful cooptation and annexation," not through military conquest, as recorded in official history, is constantly emphasized.

Much space is devoted to a description of the magnificient system of communication[14] within the Confederation; to communal economy, to education, obligatory for all inhabitants of Anauak, and to the great achievements of Anauak sages and scholars in the area of science and humanities. But above all much attention is given to descriptions of the "democratic and peaceful way" in which the Confederation was governed, to the "genuine aboriginal democracy" used in the election of governors.

Since there existed both polytheistic and monotheistic trends in the ancient Nahua religion, religious themes are treated in *Izkalotl* in a very careful and rather evasive manner. Many specific beliefs and rites are described but the issue of polytheism-monotheism, which could be ticklish in Mexico, culturally Catholic in spite of the anticlerical national ideology, is carefully avoided. Indirectly, however, this theme is touched on in articles on Nahuatl language (stressing the metaphorical character of Nahuatl), and in polemics with official historians, concerning human sacrifices apparently performed in Anauak. Due to the metaphorical character of the Nahuatl langauge—so goes the argument—many of the Nahua religious rites were misunderstood by Spaniards, and are being still misunderstood in Mexico. Though in Codices we see, indeed, pictures of the extraction of human hearts on sacrificial stones, those were only exalted poetic metaphors, reassurances directed to the Supreme Being, statements of the readiness to make even final sacrifices (not on the sacrificial stones, however) for the sake of their Father-Sun, and their own continuity dependant on solar energy.

Eulalia Guzmán, the Movement's endorsed archeologist, writes about the "Nahuatl custom of imaginary sacrifice of both adults and children in the form of paper-cut dolls, which were used during ceremonies and burned afterwards." (*Izkalotl*, September 1962)

It is impossible to give a full reinterpretation of what official historians call "the Conquest," and what the Movement's historians call "Spanish Invasion," emphasizing the temporary character of the Spanish rule over Anauak.

Only two examples of the discrepancies between the official history and the Movement's history will be presented here:

1) a) According to the simplified official history, the Aztec Empire was established mainly through the military conquest and subordination of various tribes and nations. Most conquered peoples never ac-

cepted Aztec rule, and at the first opportunity became allies of Hernan Cortés to fight with him against Aztecs.

b) The movement's History, assuming peaceful incorporation of coopted tribes and nations into the Confederation of Anauak, rejects the idea of voluntary alliances between Hernán Cortés and some of the "freely federated states of Anauak," and promotes a hypothesis of multiple and victimizing deceptions used by Cortés in regard to the peoples of Anauak.

2) a) Official history, though deploring and condemning the Conquest and particularly the tortures and assassination of "the last Aztec Emperor, Cauhtémoc," consideres the fall of Tenochtitlan as "the end of the Aztec Empire" and the beginning of Spanish rule, shaken only three centuries later, in 1810, by the War of Independence. But through those three centuries of Spanish rule natives and Spaniards mixed genetically and culturally, and thus the "new race," that of the contemporary Mexicans, was born to assume its Independence.

b) According to the Movement's history, neither the continuity of the government of the Confederation of Anauak, nor that of Nahuatl culture, was ever broken. On the eve of their great defeat (August 12/13, 1521) the members of the Anauak Great Government met officially for the last time and issued a proclamation in which they urged the people of Anauak to cultivate their culture, customs, religion, traditions until "the temporarily darkened Sun will rise again for the Great Anauak" (*Izkalotl*, June 1967).

According to the Movement's history the underground government of Anauak never stopped functioning and Nahuatl culture has been preserved secretly throughout centuries. *Izkalotl* devotes a great deal of space to the evidence of this cultural persistence, making references from time to time to the still living descendants of Cauhtémoc. In *Izkalotl* of January 1965 we find, for instance, an article illustrated with a photograph of an old man, the anniversary of whose death *Izkalotl* was commemorating. The inscription under this photograph reads: "grandson in the tenth generation of Kauhtemotzin" (the ending "tzin" being a Nahuatl reverential ending). (The spelling of "Cauhtémoc" with a "K" reflects the Movement's research on "new orthography"!)

The data on the natives' resistance, based on the current findings of the Movement's historians, have been faithfully reported in *Izkalotl*, as inspiring examples of persistence and heroism.

The day of September 25, 1949, at five minutes before two p.m. (as faithfully reported by the Mexican daily *El Universal*), became an important landmark in the making of the New History of the Movement. On that day archeologist Eulalia Guzmán discovered what she assumed to be the grave of Cauhtémoc in Ixteopan, in the state of Guerrero. This was, she announced, his grave and his bones since she found in the grave a little copper plate with the inscription "Rey e.s. Coatemo 1525 (the year of the execution of Cauhtémoc) and 1529 (the year of his funeral)." Those discoveries, to this day highly controversial, but firmly endorsed by the Movement, stimulated further historical research and produced new interpretations. The faithful companions of Cauhtémoc, who exhumed his body and transported it to his native village through the whole country, from Chiapas to Guerrero became the two new heroes of Anauak.

The contemporary situation of Anauak is diagnosed within this New History as a situation of, so to speak, stabilized occupation. The mixture of natives with Spaniards and large scale deculturation of Anauakian citizens led to grand scale confusion and identity crisis. "Spaniards" are often identified with "Europeans" who have been continuously imposing foreign, harmful elements upon the natives of *Ixachilian*, that is, America. "We are considered an underdeveloped nation but before the Spanish invasion we were among the most developed ones in the world," writes Movement-endorsed archeologist Eulalia Guzmán in the 1960 November/December issue of *Izkalotl*, "and we would have continued this way if not for those damaging foreign influences which presented themselves as civilizing and humane."

In the January/February issue of *Izkalotl* from 1961 we find a "Dialogue around Reconstruction of Anauak" in a popular column, appearing more or less regularly in this magazine.

"Does our culture exist? And if so where could it be found?" we read. "After the fall of Tenochtitlan," follows the answer, "Aztec leaders mandated that all documents should be dispersed and hidden, and that the carriers of our culture should transmit it orally to their descendants so it could be preserved this way until our times."

And we read further in the same "Dialogue":

> "Today we are people without culture, and without a fixed destiny, people who imitate, who ape others. . . . We have a colonial economy plagued by corruption. And there were times when we were a creative nation . . . our economy was autonomous and prosperous; our severe morality had made of our people a really responsible human whole. . . . We have nothing in common with the occidental culture which led Europe and the

whole world to destruction, and which was incapable of elevating human beings morally. In our Anauakian culture we have all the essential elements necessary for the moral, intellectual and spiritual elevation of mankind."

4. Ideology

Ideologies try to provide an interpretation of the past and present that will be not only acceptable to the group for which it was designed but that will build the morale of the group as well. And they try to formulate a vision of the future which will be, at the same time, obtainable and desirable to the group in question.[16] Ideologies of social movements (however critical of the larger society they may be) usually legitimize their programs and visions, not only in terms of their own (sometimes esoteric) knowledge but in terms of the official knowledge, prevalent in the larger society, as well. They recruit their members from this larger society, after all.

Most ideologies from the nineteenth century on tend to claim some scientific authority for their interpretations and predictions. The most extreme case of such a claim may be seen in Marxism, whose ideology of dialectical materialism claims to be the only "true science."

The movement of the Reappearance of Anauak, though rejecting Marxism as an "ideology unsuitable for America because of its European origin" (*Izkalotl*, December 1967) claims to be based on "scientific principles" as well, (*Izkalotl*, January 1966). The ancient Nahua sages apparently had discovered the "laws of evolution" of the Anauak Confederation based on "scientific deductions and predictions, practiced already by teachers and students in *Kalmeka*," the university of ancient Anauak. Those scholarly activities "were misunderstood by ignorant Spaniards, who assumed that *Kalmeka* was a school of wizards and sorcerers."[17]

Evolution, however, according to the Movement's assumptions, has been always subject to human control. "There is no one general plan for regulating evolution in Mexico," we read in *Izkalotl* of January/February 1967. "Its development proceeds on the basis of experiments." Those experiments are performed, apparently, with the participation of all Mexicans, collectively and "according to the spirit of aboriginal democracy" in which "every Mexican proposes a solution."

The legitimizing apparatus of the Movement's ideology of the Reappearance of Anauak is very spectacular indeed. It evokes not only the authority of both ancient Nahua and modern science, but also political rights rooted deeply in history and "continental American solidarity" as well.

Its ideological respectability is further strengthened by the emphasis on the nonviolent, revisionistic, rather than revolutionary, character of the Movement's liberating strategies. The themes of "Optimistic Evolution," "Continentalism" and "Cultural Liberation-Revisionism" come into the foreground in the Movement's ideological writings.

Optimistic Evolution Ideologists for the Movement build their view of society and of ideal human personality on the basis of what they call "the ancient Nahuatl naturalism." "*Omeyotl*, energy governed by its creator (and the source of all energy) is located in our blood," we read in *Izkalotl* of November 1963,

> and it does not ever disappear since with its disappearance the whole universe would vanish. In the moment of death *omeyotl* concentrates in the drop of blood, which goes to the source of all energy, the Sun, *Totahzin*, our glorious Father, where it purifies and activates itself in order to return to the Earth to animate another being with all the vigor of its origins and revived purity, so this new being would be superior to the previous one.

The same optimism can be seen in the application of this evolutionary principle to the history of human race. We read in *Izkalotl* of September 1960: "No human race on the road to its evolution (sometimes influenced, sometimes interrupted by other cultures) perishes permanently. Sooner or later it recovers and goes ahead again . . . Numerous peoples who had suffered for endless years of foreign domination struggle not only for their political and economic independence but for their spiritual and cultural independence from the dominant nations, as well."

And in *Izkalotl* of May 1961, Eulalia Guzmán gives Poland and China as examples of the two countries "which struggled to cultivate their own cultures in spite of being conquered by brute force."

Such assertions are usually followed by strong normative statements referring to the authority of the forefathers, and recent "revelations". They are often accompanied by specific instructions on the strategies of restoration of modernized *Nahuatl* culture and socioeconomic structure. In *Izkalotl* of January/February, 1961, we read one of the numerous "Proclamations to Mexicans," issued by the Movement's founder Rodolfo Nieva. This particular Proclamation contains most of the legitimizing arguments (references to Anauak's destiny, mission, overcoming of painful alienation and recent "revelations" by the "bearers of tradition") and because of its importance it is translated here in its totality.

"Proclamation to Mexicans"

"Fellow-countrymen, I make this appeal with all my heart to implore you to keep in mind your condition of subservience; your very existence having been overwhelmed by an alien way of life imposed by these Spaniards; a regime from which you are still powerless to deliver yourselves.

I hereby appeal to you to strive for liberation from this foreign tyranny, and resurrect your true fatherland, the Great Confederation of Anauak.

Believe me when I tell you that you exist in a state of alienation, knowing neither who you are nor whence you came, unconscious not only of your true needs, but also of your destination. It is imperative that you recognize the resurrection of the Great Confederation of Anauak as your duty and your destiny. Only through this mandate, inherited from our progenitors can we aspire to the dignity of true sons of Mexico.

Mexicans, no such appellation has reached your ears before this day—deafened as you are by the verbiage of foreigners.

Now, Mexicans, we have at last heard the revelation from the lips of our brethren, the true bearers of our traditions. Our eyes have opened to the truths concerning our people's fate, and this enlightenment we now share with you that you may use to the full the implications of this knowledge.[18]

This appeal directed to the followers and potential followers of the Movement is formulated in an antiquated Spanish, which in spite of being so condemned as a "foreign language" adds solemnity to this neo-Nahua Proclamation.

Communal spirit, sometimes called "Nahua Altruism," and constantly opposed to "European type of egotistic individualism," is emphasized as the essential characteristic of the ideal Nahua personality type. Both respect for native traditions, and openmindedness, combined with ability to experiment in various ways, and to be flexible and tolerant, are emphasized as additional characteristics required of twentieth century inhabitants of Anauak.

In comparison, however, with the strong elaboration of the themes of socioeconomic and political reconstruction, the emphasis on ideal personality is not very strong in the ideology of the Movement. Unlike the highly individualistic contemporary Mexican, the future citizen of Anauak is supposed to be above all a deeply social man, respectful of traditions and subordinated to the will of a democratic majority. He is to be sober, disciplined, obedient. His knowledge and efforts are not to serve his personal glorification but the well-being of society.

People in revived Anauak "should live close to each other like the fingers of a human hand—an old Nahua principle," we read in the "Declaration of Principles of the Party of Mexicanity" in the 1968 June issue of *Izkalotl*.

Continentalism The Movement of the Reappearance of Anauak because of its emphasis on the distinction between "pure Nahuas" and "mixed-blood Nahuas," could be easily classified as a racist ideology. It seems, however, that in spite of some racist accents, this ideology is predominantly of a continental type, somewhat similar to hellenistic ideology. The distinction between "pure Nahuas," called most often "pure race Mexicans," and "mixed-blood Nahuas," called "racially mixed Mexicans," is spelled out in more detail in an article "Mexicanity" in *Izkalotl* of February 1964. "The Mexican of a pure race" we read in this article, "is a carrier of Mexican culture. The Mexican of a mixed-race is racially Mexican and mentally Spanish-European." It is evident that the term "race" is used here ambiguously: sometime it means "race;" sometimes "culture" (as this term is used, as well, in the plain Mexican-Spanish).

A "Mexican of a mixed race," we read further in the same article "should Mexicanize himself as soon as possible. He should learn Nahuatl, develop a liking for corn instead of bread, prefer articles made in Mexico to those made abroad, associate fraternally with other Mexicans and restore the Mexican type community."

And in *Izkalotl* of January 1967 we read even more detailed "Instructions for the Members of the Movement" from which we learn that all members should:

1. use the symbol of the Movement *Nani Ollin* (Time-Evolution)
2. speak a Mexican language
3. adopt Mexican names
4. give Mexican names to children
5. celebrate all civil acts first according to Mexican rites, then according to the laws.
6. combat all vices, especially those of foreign origin
7. organize their homes according to Mexican customs
8. convert all relatives to Mexicanity especially children.

It has to be emphasized that the term "Mexican," though understood by the members of the movement as "Nahuatl" or "Nahua," may be uasily understood by an uninitiated Mexican reader in the sense of Mexican (mestizo) national. Some passages of *Iskalotl*, if read superficially may be, indeed, understood as assertions of rather typical Mexican nationalism. This ambiguity had gained, probably, many members to the Movement of Reappearance of Anauak!

Though the distinction between "pure race Mexicans" and "mixed-race Mexicans" is so often repeated in *Izkalotl*, the members of the Movement defend themselves strongly against any imputation of racism. In *Izkalotl* of August 1961 we read such an energetic protest: "We are not racists! We accept as Anaukians all those born under the sky of Anauak, independently of where their ancestors came from!" This is certainly a broad and non-racist definition of Anauakian citizenship.

Most people of the ancient Anauak, apparently, were bilingual, speaking both their native language and Nahuatl, the official language of the Confederation. A similar solution is also advocated by the Movement for the revived Anauak. After the Spanish language is eliminated as a national language, everybody in Anauak will be speaking both Nahuatl (restored as a national language) and the language of his own aboriginal group. The Confederation of Anauak will extend, according to their predictions, from Alta California (now in the United States) to Nicaragua, as she did before the Spanish invasion, and she may eventually embrace all of the American continent.

"There exist some vestiges of Nahua culture even as far as Alaska," we read in *Izkalotl* of October 1962 and one of the Movement's ideologists claims that in spite of the fact that

> our states had chosen to organize themselves as monarchies, those monarchies always had a democratic parliamentary character and functioned on the basis of popular voting. All types of Republics, such as we see today, with their Parliaments and Assemblies, are in fact of Aztec origin, similar to those which existed in Nikarahua, the country of Nikira (Aztekah), in Tlaxallan, and the same which existed during the first years after the foundation of Tenochtitlan.[19]

Such traditions, it is assumed, may help in further consolidation of the American continent under the leadership of Nahuas.

According to *Mexicayotl*,[20] the Movement's sacred philosophical book, there exists evidence of even further expansion of the ancient

Anauak's influence on the American continent. Some preliminary conversations were, apparently, conducted between Anauak and Inca governments with a view towards federation of those two most powerful states in America.

The continental appeals are spread throughout all issues of *Izkalotl* and the "Sister Nations of the Continent" are called to restore their native cultures, and promised the Movement's "fraternal cooperation" and participation in all efforts and struggles. Anauak, an enormous modernized Confederation, (led in the past by Nahuas, and to be led by the Nahuas in the future) is supposed to "reappear," or "re-emerge," to be "revived" or "restored," according to Movement terminology, maybe, even during the lifetime of some of the Movement's leaders.

The revelations of ancient Nahuas, the "laws of evolution," the approaching cataclysm[21] and the efforts of the Movement's members are presented by the Movement's ideologists as strong arguments for this prophetic prediction.

Cultural Liberation-Revisionism The action undertaken by the Movement of Reappearance of Anauak is sometimes referred to as "The Third Movement of Liberation," the War of Independence (1810) and Mexican Revolution (1910) being the first two. The cultural character of this liberation is strongly emphasized in all ideological writings, side by side with its usefulness to contemporary Mexico. We read in a 1965 issue of *Izkalotl* the following "Message to the Country" issued by the Movement's leader Rodolfo Nieva:

> Reconstruction of our Mexican culture, as an evolutionary norm for our country is:
> 1. obligation toward our forefathers
> 2. the right (to have our own culture)
> 3. necessity (in order to overcome underdevelopment and corruption).

"The languages Nahuatl and Maya," we read in an April 1962 issue of *Izkalotl*, "are like Greek and Latin for Europe. They prove the common origin of American nations. All American languages have Nahuatl and Maya as their basis."

Though reintroduction of Nahuatl as a national language is given a strong priority in the cultural reconstruction, the reintroduction of selected and modernized Nahua customs and structural elements is given a strong emphasis as well. In the September 1960 issue of *Izkalotl* we read about necessary "efforts to revive all positive, socio-philosophical and political aspects of Anauak culture without ignoring the contributions of the occidental culture but giving priority to native traditions as a basis of our nationality. These native values are distinctive for our race and give her its personality."

Both communism and occidental capitalism are described as unsuitable for the revived Anauak. In an August 1961 issue of *Izkalotl* we find strong condemnations of those two systems by the Movement. Communism is condemned for:

1. imposing its system with terror and violence upon other countries
2. centralism and concentration of power in the hands of the few
3. annihilation of human dignity.

While occidental capitalism is condemned for:

1. its egotistic individualism
2. decadent system (with germs of self-destruction).

Like other aspects of the culture planned for the revived Anauak, the political culture of this Confederation is supposed to have a strong aboriginal basis but at the same time it is supposed to be eclectic and open. "According to Mexican naturalism, (*Izkalotl* of December 1967) "society is a natural phenomenon, based on human sentiments." Israeli *kibbutzim*, "inspired by Mexican *kalpullis*," are described as ideologically most compatible with the political style planned for Anauak. (*Izkalotl*, September 1960, "Left or Right? No! Mexicanity!")

Though both communism and capitalism are condemned, the Movement of Reappearance of Anauak is ready to experiment with any cultural and political style which is compatible with its basic ideals, and to ally sometimes with the Right, sometimes with the Left, always in accordance with the basic interests of Anauak.

Democratic social structure with its emphasis on open discussion of the issues, grass-roots ideology, nonviolent resistance (Ghandi style) and revisionistic, nonrevolutionary strategies is strongly preferred to all other systems but reinterpreted and "Nahuaised" in the usual Movement style. "In our old native culture (May 1963 issue of *Izkalotl*) we find the basis of real democracy in which wealth, power and work are distributed equally. This democracy is rooted in *kalpulli* communal but not communistic organization in which capital is formed through surplus production and collective savings."

I was acutely aware of those ideological themes during the whole day excursion to which I was invited by the Movement on the occasion of the Aztec New Year December 22, 1974. After about three hours two buses filled with the Movement's members had arrived in a picturesque *rancho* in the midst of Nahuatl-speaking highlands. We were greeted by the *rancho* owner, an old Mexican revolutionary in a large Zapata-like hat, and by dozens of Indians from the area. Since I did much research in Mexico among both rural mestizos and Indians this setting was rather familiar to me, and I could well imagine the daily life of those highland farmers who did not wear their Indian garments anymore but had probably preserved some degree of Nahua identity, and some amount of Nahuatl culture. They were obviously poor, some of them probably owners of small pieces of this hilly sterile land, many younger ones were certainly landless and struggling hard to maintain their families through hired work in the area and in distant Mexico where they were more humiliated but usually a little less exploited.

I observed with curiosity the contacts between those rural Nahuas and the neo-Nahua intellectuals from the Movement of Reappearance of Anauak. The interaction between those two different groups was certainly very different from any interaction between Indians and non-Indians, or between any educated and non-educated people, I had ever observed before in my life. There was some sense of a respectful distance between them but, at the same time, obvious mutual confidence and a strong atmosphere of mutual expectations. I had just observed the neo-Aztec ceremony of Assignment of Names and had a chance to see with what intensity those local people watched their own old customs staged so carefully and solemnly by the members of the Movement. They obviously expected much of such learning of their own past, and probably there was something which the Movement members wanted to learn from them as well. Though I could imagine this mutual learning, I could equally well imagine how their mutual expectations could be bitterly disappointed in the future.

Our host took us all on a mountain-climbing tour of his *Rancho* and he showed us his meager vegetable plots and various orchards of young peach and apple trees growing from the stony dry earth. All over his *rancho* we could also see hundreds of small fruit trees planted in various containers. He was trying to teach everybody around, he explained, how to grow trees and vegetables so they could survive "when the Great Disaster predicted for our era of Aquarius" would descend upon them. I wondered what they assumed would happen to them after this Great Disaster. There would be no landless people among them anymore—this would likely be their first vision—and nobody would call them "Indians," a term so offensive to them. Everybody around, and in the towns as well, would be speaking Nahuatl, like those guests from Mexico who try to speak it (but surely much better). They would have nice fiestas with fireworks, and they would not have to hide their saints and "idols" anymore . . .

5. Social Structure of the Movement

A. Dual Character   According to the articles published in *Iskalotl* the ideology of the Movement has been implemented through a variety of organizations. In order to understand those organizations one has to emphasize again the Movement's basic duality. The Movement of Reappearance of Anauak is a semi-secret political sect,[22] which emerged in a modern, democratic, occidental but still strongly post-colonial society at a moment of economic and political unrest and enlarged contacts with the larger world. But since the main objective of the Movement is the revival of the culture and, eventually, the political organization of the ancient Nahua Confederation, and since this process of revival is to happen within the occidental society, the Movement has to operate on two levels, occidental and non-occidental. This is particularly difficult since due to its revisionistic nonviolent strategies both the cultural and political Nahuaization of Mexico is to occur gradually.

The leaders of the Movement are themselves culturally Mexicans— they are only ideologically Nahuas. In order to maintain the Movement, they must deal with both the "uninitiated" Mexican elites, and the largely deculturated rural Nahuas. They act as Mexicans on some occasions, and as Nahuas on others. Because of the secrecy and vagueness resulting from their dual operations, it is sometimes difficult to distinguish the ideological from the real, to draw the line between their dreams, plans and accomplishments, or even to assess the number of leaders and converts to the Movement. They claim many thousands of followers not only in Mexico but within the American continent since the Movement is to have a continental scope. But among those Movement's members and leaders are those who "returned to nature" (those who died), and while speaking and writing about them the mystical language of "revelations," "intuitions" and communication" is used. The deceased Movement's leader, Rodolfo Nieva, and the last Aztec ruler, Cauhtémoc, are among those who "returned to nature" but nevertheless "keep coming" to the Movement's meetings.

The ambiguity in the Spanish language of such terms as *gobierno*, which may mean both the government of the country and the executive committee of a voluntary organization and such terms as *Presidente*, which may mean either President of the country or chairman, help greatly in this dual functioning of the Movement.

    B. Structure   In Table I, presented below, I try to show this basic

Table I

Formal Organizations of the Movement of Reappearance of Anauak

Movement's Units:

Nahua largely sacred	occidental largely secular

1. Great Government of
    Anauak (*Ueyitlahtohkan*)
	Presidium of the Association
	    of the Reappearance of
	    Anauak

        a. monthly *Izkalotl*

        b. Party of Mexicanity
          (*Partido de Mexicanidad*)

  2. Institute of the Investigation of the Culture of Anauak
        a. Academy of Anauak Law
        b. Academy of the Mexican (Nahuatl) Language
        c. Academy of Anauak Philosophy
        d. Academy of Anauak Art
        e. Academy of Anauak Dance
        f. Academy of Anauak Literature
        g. Academy of Anauak Song
        h. Academy of Anauak Sculpture
        i. Academy of Biological Sciences
        j. Academy of Ethnohistory

3. Nahua University:
   Kalmekatl or *Calmécac*

4. First Reconstructed *Ixkalpulli*   District
        a. rural *Calpulli's*
        b. urban *Calpulli's*

        5. associated organizations
    Federation of Students from San Luis Potosi

        6. foreign representations:
    ambassadors of the Movement in America

duality of the Movement's organizations. On the right side of the dividing line are the secular, occidental names of the Movement's organizations and the names of the secular branches of the Movement, which do not have their Nahua counterparts. On the left side are non-occidental, sacred Nahua units, whenever possible with their Nahuatl names. Cutting across the line are those Movement's units which function both as sacred and secular, Nahua and national Mexican at the same time.

C. Activities Since the Movement is still relatively young and its small inner circle has remained very dynamic, all activities of its numerous organizations are carried out under the auspices of *Ueyitlahtohkan* (Great Government) itself and are amply documented in *Izkalotl*.

Table II

Activities of the Movement of the Reappearance of Anauak

(i) goal-directed	(ii) research	(iii) consolidatory	(iv) political and diplomatic
a) aiming at cultural reconstruction b) aiming at socioeconomic reconstruction		a) recruitment b) maintenance c) communication d) legitimation	a) directed toward increasing of the Movement's power in Mexico b) lobbying for governmental decrees and actions c) directed toward Movement's defense

(i) goal-directed activities
a) activities aiming at cultural reconstruction
Cultural reconstruction is to come before the political restructuring of Mexican society, and it is considered the Movement's most important objective. There exist special units within the Movement devoted entirely to the teaching of Nahua culture and language: various courses, workshops, round tables, conferences and congresses are organized for the purpose of promoting and teaching Nahua culture. The great dream of the Movement leaders is the eventual transformation of the National University of Mexico (UNAM) into a modernized

Kalmekatl[23] the ancient Nahua institution of higher learning (*Izkalotl*, May 1961). I do not know to what extent and in what form *Kalmekatl* was revived by the Movement since I was able to find only one reference to it in *Izkalotl* (May 1961). During the ceremony of Assignment of Names (*Asignación de Nombres*) to which I was invited, I noticed, however that some men from the Movement wore tiny red strings in their hair. I asked about the significance of those strings and was told that these men were students and teachers of *Kalmekatl*, and was further informed that all four of the young men who were assigned Aztec names during this ceremony had had to study previously in *Kalmekatl* in order to be eligible recipients of those names.

Such assignments of Aztec names and many other old Nahua ceremonies such as Nahua weddings or celebration of various holidays according to the Aztec Calendar are among important attempts at cultural reconstruction. One finds also in *Izkalotl* notes on the celebration of various anniversaries, such as the anniversary of the fall of Tenochtitlan or the victory of Cuitlahuac over Cortés (renamed from the Spanish *Noche Triste*, "Sad Night," to "Glorious Night" or "Victorious Night" stressing thus the difficult victory of the Aztecs over the Spaniards).

A note from the August, 1963 issue of *Izkalotl* gives the flavor of those celebrations: in an article entitled "Magnificent Supper of the Assembly," we read that this annual supper took place "with the assistance of distinguished journalists and many eminent persons from intellectual, governmental and diplomatic circles." The supper was served in a large *patio* of the Mexican Club of Journalists and in the same place "a magnificent ceremony was organized to celebrate the Glorious Night in which heroic Kuitlauak[24] defeated Hernán Cortés, June 30, 1520." We read further that on this occasion the Movement's Academy of Anauak Law was inaugurated and diplomas were distributed to its founders.

b) activities aimed at socioeconomic reconstruction

The most important among these activities is a large-scale (as presented in *Izkalotl*) founding of precolonial-type *calpulli's* (or *kalpulli's*)[25] mainly in rural or semi-rural areas around Mexico City but also to a lesser extent in cities and towns. Some of those *calpullis* are newly founded (the group of neighbors—peasants largely Nahuatl-speaking or of Nahua origin—being invited to organizational meetings by the leaders of the Movement), some of them are established through a restructuring of the existing organizations.

Some of those *calpulli's* are more similar to precolonial ones, mainly *calpulli's* made out of *ejidos*,[26] others, for instance, landless rural and urban ones, bear little similarity, indeed, to precolonial *calpulli's*. In all cases, however, the Movement's leaders inject into new *calpulli's* the Movement's ideology, inspire and press its members to learn Nahuatl, to revive Nahua customs, to organize Nahua ceremonies and to participate in various activities of the Movement. "*Kalpulli*," we read in *Izkalotl* of April 1962, "is the basic institution which offers the greatest guarantee of good life in Anauak. This is our own form of democracy and its revival will liberate our country from decadence." The hopes related to the reconstruction of the *calpulli* system are spelled out in more detail in the same editorial. Due to its social organization, ideally communal (but not communistic, as it is emphasized at every step), ownership of land, involvement in all sorts of communal labors by a relatively small group of neighbors well-acquainted with one another, and Council of Elders (*Consejo de Prudentes*, in Spanish, *Tlahtokan*, in Nahuatl) elected directly by the people, the *calpulli* system gives the best guarantee against the rising of authoritarian leaders (*cacigasgo*), and abuse of authority. Through its economic structure, based in communal projects, the *calpulli* system eliminates the intermediaries (*acapadores*) that plague the nation. "Both social justice and national security depend, indeed, on the reconstruction of the *kalpulli* system," concludes the editorial.

Much space is taken in *Izkalotl* by popular historical articles, describing precolonial *calpulli's*, by suggestions in regard to their revival, and by descriptions of the events related to the founding of the new *calpulli's*.

Besides economic and political legitimations of those "neo-*calpullis*," strong traditional legitimations are constantly stressed. According to a note which appeared in the October 1972 issue of *Izkalotl*, a book written by the Movement's key historian, Ignacio Romerovargas, *Political Organization of the Peoples of Anauak*,[27] was just translated into Chinese, and "according to a letter to the author from Mao, *kalpulli's* served him as a model for establishment of Chinese communes."

Another Mexican scholar, an archeologist, Eulalia Guzman, considered one of the Movement's key ideologists in spite of not being of Nahua origin,[28] in her article "Practical functioning of *kalpulli*" published in *Izkalotl* of October 1962, makes the following statement about the possibility of the revival of this precolonial institution: "It is quite possible, within the framework of our constitutional law, to reestablish *kalpulli* within any small or medium traditional village. It is important that such an organization (of private character and with a name, let's say, like "Civic and Cultural Association") be modeled on the old *kalpulli*." She then gives concrete suggestions on how one could work within those *calpulli's* on "revival, progress and growth of the culture of Anauak in all its various aspects under the circumstances imposed by contemporary life." In *Izkalotl* of November 1961 there is an interesting description of the founding and consequent anniversary celebration of the first *calpulli* established by the Movement.

> Two years ago, May 28, 1959, the first *kalpulli* of the Movement of Reappearance of Anauak was founded in the area of Xochimilco, D. F. Invited by the leaders of the Movement a group of enthusiastic neighbors of real Mexican race and spirit, gathered in a house of Doctor X. They elected their *Tlahtokan* (Governing Council) in order to create the first *kalpulli* which designated Professor Y as executive director and Professor Z as director.[29] Today—two years from its founding, the *kalpulli* has a magnificent secondary school, the product of this *kalpulli's* efforts. In order to celebrate the *kalpulli's* second anniversary the Movement's leaders met with the members of *kalpulli's Tlahtokan* (Governing Council) on the top of the hill of *Tentli*, (God's Path) where the sages of Anauak used to meet to discuss Nahua science. The members of *Tlahtokan* performed there their ceremonial vows to accomplish faithfully their mission. We were accompanied during this moving ceremony by many *kalpulli's* neighbors and, finally a magnificent meal was served in the house of Doctor X.

The April 1962 issue of *Izkalotl* announces enthusiastically that the *calpulli's* 1, 2, 3, 4 and 5 "had confederated" thus establishing the first *ixkalpulli* (district) under the auspices of the Movement. This was, according to *Izkalotl* "a very important step toward the economic reconstruction of Anauak." In the same issue of *Izkalotl* the following vision of this reconstruction is outlined: "*Kalpulli* without losing the characteristics of its autonomy and self-sufficiency associates with other *kalpullis* of Anauak and recognizes the authority of its directive organs such as *Ixkalpulli* (district), *Tekuyotl* (state) and *Ueytlahtokayotl* (Great Government)."

Though presented in such a matter-of-fact manner, this is, indeed, a great revisionistic vision, inspired by solid research on old Anauak. "Working peacefully through grass-roots organization of *kalpulli's*," continues the article, "the old Nahua democracy will be slowly in-

jected into all Nahuatl-renamed and reconstructed Mexican administrative institutions and, eventually, the leader of the Movement will
be installed as the *Ueytlahtokayotl*, President of the Great Government." In this way the Mexican Republic will be peacefully transformed into a modernized Confederation of Anauak.

Simultaneously with these efforts at reestablishment of the *calpulli*
system, the Movement, through its Party of Mexicanity *(Partido de
Mexicanidad)*, plans to take over the Presidency of Mexico by parlia-
mentary means. The Party of Mexicanity has been preparing to
eventually enter the presidential elections, as an equal rival with other
parties, a somewhat unrealistic idea, indeed, within the *de facto* one-
party Mexican political system.

(ii) research activities

Since, according to the creed of the Movement, the administration
of ancient Anauak was based on "scientific principles" ("unlike that
of the Spanish Empire"), the emphasis on research is very strong within this political sect. This research, mainly archeological, linguistic
and historical, is done both by the scholars of the Movement and by its
sympathizers. It is hard to assess to what extent the multiple Academies
(see Table I) established by the Movement do function as research
institutes, and to what extent they reflect only the Movement's aspirations. From time to time some references to conferences sponsored by
those Academies can be found in *Izkalotl*, and we can read there as
well about those Academies' ceremonial inaugurations. The names
of founders, directors and some collaborators of the Academies are
also published on the pages of *Izkalotl*. The oldest of those Academies,
the Academy of Nahuatl Language and the Academy of Anauk Law,
we learn from *Izkalotl*, are very well-connected with contemporary
Mexican national society. We read in *Izkalotl* of August 1963, that
the Academy of Anauak Law was established in 1963 under the auspices of the Mexican Bar Association (probably at the time when the
Movement's leader was president of this Association), while the
Academy of Nahuatl Language established cooperation with the
National University of Mexico (UNAM) *(Izkalotl,* September, 1960).
The Academy of Law has been working on the problem of how Nahua
Law could be revived in Mexico *(Izkalotl* November 1969). It even
issued suggestions, condensed into twelve points, for going about
such a revival. In *Izkalotl* of November/December 1960 we read about
an important reunion of the Academy of Nahuatl Language in which
the standardization of the Nahuatl alphabet was established by the

members of this Academy. Several books were published under the auspices of the Institute for the investigation of the Culture of Anauak.[30] Lists of the books in which precolonial history is distorted[31] and those books approved by the Movement[32] are published from time to time in *Izkalotl*.

Under the auspices of the Institute for Investigation of the Culture of Anauak, four Anauak Congresses were organized, some of them being sponsored by the specific Academies. Thus from the *Izkalotl* of April 1964 we learn that the First Congress of Nahuatl Language took place from April 24-26, and that it formulated the declaration that "the people of Tlaxcala (in the Confederation of Anauak) were not traitors (as it is assumed in official history) but the victims of Hernán Cortés who deceived them." This proclamation is a good example of the ways in which the Movement tries to "eliminate the falsities from pre-Kuauhtemic history."

Many other pronouncements have been issued on the occasion of various Congresses and under the auspices of various Academies. At these congresses all sorts of decisions are announced, among them a project to increase the number of issues of *Izkalotl* to sixty-five hundred copies "with the final goal of transforming it into a daily publication."[33] It is interesting to note that this announcement was published at the time when, one year after the death of the Movement's founder and leader, its activities had probably diminished and *Izkalotl* itself started appearing less regularly than before.

Much research has been done by various Academies on ancient Nahua ceremonies and such findings are almost immediately disseminated through *Izkalotl*, and through various conferences and talks on both academic and popular levels. I had an opportunity to see an elaborate gadget (constructed by one of the Movement's members, a mechanical engineer) in which a coordination of the Aztec with the Gregorian Calendar was made in such a way that one could easily find out which day of the Aztec Calendar corresponded to which day of the Gregorian Calendar.

(iii) consolidatory activities

Consolidatory activities are necessary in any formal organization and even more important in a political sect with such great aspirations, as the Movement of Reappearance of Anauak. They consist of all those activities which assure the growth of the organization, maintain its functioning, assure communication among the members and with the larger world, legitimate its actions and provide symbols and myths. As noted by Bruce Cameron[34] the life cycles of some of the social movements are equivalent to the life cycles of their founders, and this could have easily happened with this particular Movement whose founder and leader, Rodolfo Nieva, died in 1969. Though the Movement was temporarily weakened after the death of Rodolfo Nieva, (especially its most secular branch, that of the Party of Mexicanity), it was revived, and maybe even strengthened, with the addition of the myth of its deceased leader who "returned to nature," and along with other Nahua heroes, "has been helping ever since the cause of Reappearance of Anauak." But such a post mortem charisma would not have been sufficient to maintain a movement which was not previously legitimized through the powerful symbols of sacred Nahua tradition, and strongly anchored in contemporary Mexican society due to the prominence and contacts of its leader.

Every issue of *Izkalotl* gives us evidence of the strong consolidatory activities of the Movement.

The Table III shown below is to serve as a visual aid to understanding of the Movement's recruiting activities from among the eligible population.

TABLE III

Pure-Nahuas		Mixed-Nahuas	
educated	non-educated	educated	non-educated
- +	- +	- +	- +

The distinction between "pure Nahuas" and "mixed Nahuas" is assumed to refer to genetic rather than cultural purity. Though ambiguous in most of the contexts, it seems that within their inner circles those terms are rather clear, and the term "pure Nahuas" means "direct descendants of the ancient Nahuas," most highly esteemed by the Movement as being "the carriers of old tradition."

The signs "+" and "-" refer to possession of traditional Nahua culture. Those indicated by "+" are culturally as Nahua as is possible in contemporary Mexico. Those who are marked with "-" are culturally most de-Nahuaised. Those inbetween the two poles possess various grades and types[35] of Nahua culture.

There exists an intense contact between leaders of the Movement (most of them "neo-Nahua," as I like to think of them, since independently of their genetic heritage, they learned only as adults both Nahuatl language and some Nahua culture) and the "real Nahuas." Some of these Nahua Indians are still monolingual, and, apparently, descendants of the ancient families, often isolated in the distant mountains and, apparently, possessors not only of the "intact Nahua culture" but of the sacred secrets of the last Aztec elites as well. To those "real Nahuas" the "neo-Nahuas" make pilgrimages to learn from them as much as possible, and to incorporate them into the Movement.

Most of the Movement's recruitment has been done, so far as I was able to assess, either among young college students or among rural Nahuas living on the outskirts of Mexico City.

I attended a couple of such "recruitment sessions" on the occasion of the lectures given to college students by one of the Movement's leaders. The slides of the best archeological monuments of the ancient Nahuas were shown during those sessions and the films of the pilgrimages to "sacred places" and to Nahuatl-speaking natives, "carriers of ancient Nahua culture", made by their contemporary descendants, were displayed and discussed. The students were told that they should be very proud of being themselves descendants of the ancient Nahua astronomers, sages and poets. All their questions were carefully noted, and their addresses were taken at the end of the lecture. They were informed that they would receive the answers to their questions, as well as "the messages" sent to their home addresses.

Numerous courses in Nahuatl, ranging from kindergarten to university level, serve as recruiting techniques to the Movement as well. I had only a short glimpse of the teaching techniques for children; and of their examination in Nahuatl language with many proud parents watching this performance. Even on the basis of this one session, however, I could well imagine how difficult it would be to convert culturally occidental Mexican adults into the poetic, metaphorical way of thinking so characteristic of ancient Nahuas. With children this task is considerably easier since metaphorical thinking is not yet lost among them.

The re-Nahuaisation of uneducated rural people of Nahua origin has been accomplished, it seems, mainly through the sympathetic correcting of their still partially Nahua customs and ceremonies, and the revival of their old *calpulli* system.

I had the opportunity to attend one such carefully researched and staged old Nahua ceremony of Assignment of Names (*Asignación de Nombres*), and could well see with what tremendous reverence and emotion this ceremony was observed by the dozens of rural Nahuas who were invited to participate.

Calpullis, the basic units of old Nahuas' social organization, have been energetically introduced mainly to suburban communities with Nahuatl-speaking population by the Movement's leaders. Some of those new *calpullis* have land, some of them do not.[36] Formal organization of those new *calpullis* is based on ancient Nahua models, and its members are taught how to solve their modern problems in a "communal way" through the "aboriginal democratic debates." They are also taught ancient ceremonies to be practiced in their *calpullis*.

A good example of another type of consolidating activity may be found in a "Note on the Fourth Congress of Mexicanity," (*Izkalotl*, March/August/May, 1967) during which the "Movement's song," called "Mexicanity," was issued. "This song," we read, "is not an anthem, however, since (a) anthems have foreign, not Nahua, musical composition, and (b) anthems have a military spirit, and destructive themes, while the Movement is dedicated only to the constructive activities of restoration of Anauak." We see in this note a combination of a strong emphasis on the traditional cultural style (as seen by the Movement's leaders) with strong emphasis on the contemporary non-violent social style, influenced by Ghandi, who is greatly admired by the Movement's leaders.

The recruitment to the Movement did not stop with the death of its leader. New *calpulli's* have been organized, Nahua ceremonies have multiplied, and the sense of a mystical bond within the Movement was rather strengthened, it seems, through a belief that its founder and leader has been "purifying himself in nature," and, thus, "being in communication with the Nahua forefathers," has been accumulating his energies in order to return to the earth and to participate even more fully in activities aimed at the Reappearance of Anauak. The assertion of the continuity of the Aztec Government had been not only maintained but even strengthened through continuous historical research.

The "scientific" and "experimental" character of the Movement has been stressed side by side with its traditional and mystical character. Concern with modernization, economic development, ecology, political neutrality (combined with an emphasis on borrowing from all cultures and political systems), have been claimed by the Movement side by side with the assertions of the superiority of Anauak

institutions, the superiority of Anauak material culture (as compared
to Spanish culture of the sixteenth century), the aristocratic character
of the Nahua race, and its political strategy of "the peaceful cooptation and annexing, prevalent in old Anauak." And it is repeated over
and over again in *Izkalotl* that according to ancient Nahua prophecies
the revived Anauak Confederation is to assume soon its leadership
over the whole American continent.

(iv) political and diplomatic activities

The Movement's political and diplomatic activities may be roughly
divided into

a) those which are mainly directed toward increasing the Movement's power in Mexico

b) those which are mainly directed toward lobbying for governmental decress and actions leading to restoration of Anauak, and

c) those which are directed toward the Movement's defense.

The most important secular arm of the Movement is its Party of
Mexicanity (*Partido de Mexicanidad*) founded on September 15, 1965,
which has been working to be recognized as eligible to enter presidential elections. Its final goal is winning the office of the President
of Mexico for the Movement's leader, *Tlakantektzinli* of Tenochtitlan-
Mexico. According to the Manifesto issued by the National Organizational Commission of the Party of Mexicanity, the main goals of the
Party are:

1) To revive the Mexican Race which consists of (a) pure native
   Mexicans, (b) Mexicans of mixed-blood, and (c) all those who
   live in this country.
2) To establish Mexican philosophy (as a basis for the interpretation of the world). Its first function will be elimination of
   the corruption widespread in the country.
3) Restructuring of the Nation.
   a) all Mexicans are to enjoy sufficient social welfare.
   b) only Mexican people would control functioning of public
      power.
4) To summarize: the Party is trying to carry out the high cultural
   mission assigned to us by our Destiny. (*Izkalotl*, September/
   October 1965)

In this document the duality, so typical of this Movement, is clearly
seen in spite of the ambiguity of the terminology. The appeals are
made to the Movement's members and to the Mexican Nation as a
whole. The term "Mexican" may mean either "the citizen of the

Mexican Republic" or "the native Nahua." The appeals in terms of "reconstruction of the nation," "sufficient social welfare for all," "elimination of corruption from public life," and the "control by Mexican people of the functioning of public power" can be, certainly, endorsed both by the members of the Movement and by the average Mexican as well.

Some pronouncements of the Party are much more specific. In *Izkalotl* of November/December 1965 we read, for instance, about the ways in which the new Party of Mexicanity is "superior" to other Mexican parties.

1. It is superior to *PRI*, (the Party in power) "since *PRI*, though it unified all revolutionaries (from the 1910 Revolution) and in this way realized its mission, did not manage, however, to assure the economic independence of the country, and did not develop philosophical doctrines congruent with the history, traditions and the Destiny of our People."
2. PAN (*Partido de Acción Nactional* - Party of National Action, a largely Catholic party)—"lacks doctrine completely and it is at the service of the right-wing foreign interests."
3. PPS (*Partido Socialista Popular* - Peoples' Socialistic Party), "has a foreign political doctrine."
4. PARM (*Partido de la Revolución Mexicana*, Party of the Mexican Revolution, a party of old Mexican revolutionaries), "has all our respect but it lacks a doctrine."

In *Izkalotl* of October/November 1966 we find a note that the Party of Mexicanity "already organized seven electoral districts in the metropolitan area," and then we read another little note that the Party "proposes elimination of administrative divisions into *ayuntamientos*, institutions of foreign, colonial origin which never really functioned in Mexico, and proposes replacement of *ayuntamientos by kalpullis*."

Though some of this lobbying for the restoration of Anauak institutions and culture has been done through the Party of Mexicanity, most of the activities leading to Reappearance of Anauak continue to be sponsored by other units of the Movement such as the monthly magazine *Izkalotl* or various Academies. Many letters, for instance, to the President of Mexico have been published in *Izkalotl*, some of them with requests, others with protests. In the October 1962 issue of *Izkalotl* we find a letter to President Lopez Mateos asking him in the name of the Movement for (a) restoration of old lakes in the Valley of Mexico, and (b) reintroduction of Nahuatl language into Mexican schools.

In the May 1966 issue of *Izkalotl*, a letter to the President is published in which the Movement asks him for implementation of the old decree according to which February 28th should be declared a Day of National Mourning to commemorate the execution of the heroic defender of Tenochtitlan, the last ruler of the Confederation of Anauak, Cauhtemoc, by Hernan Cortes.

In the June 1965 issue of *Izkalotl,* we read about an ambitious project of repatriation from Chicago to Mexico of "all Nahuas residing in that city."

Numerous protest letters published in *Izkalotl* are examples of defense activities characteristic of all social movements but, probably, even more intense in those which try to revindicate the rights of native people, as does the Movement of Reappearance of Anauak.

In the January 1967 issue of *Izkalotl* we read a letter of protest against the memorial table which was placed in the *Plaza de las Tres Culturas,* in the section Tlatelolco of Mexico City. The inscription on this memorial table, which so offended the members of the Movement is, in fact, the most condensed expression of the current Mexican national identity. It says: "On August 13th 1521 Tlatelolco heroically defended by Kauhtemoc, fell into the hands of Hernan Cortes. This was neither a victory nor a defeat but the painful birth of contemporary Mexico."

While condemning this memorial table, the Movement in the same article condemns a monument of Charles IV, as well. "This inscription," says the article, "and the monument of Charles IV are an insult for Mexicans who remember well the slavery of which they were victims during more than three centuries. For this reason they should both disappear." Nothing more is said in this particular article about the reasons for rejection of the inscription on the table. Such reasons should be, however, by now self-evident to the readers of this book. Since for the members of the Movement the defeat of Tenochtitlan was the greatest defeat in Anauak history, it could not be seen by them as a "painful birth of contemporary Mexico."

In the November issue of *Izkalotl* we find a protest letter to the President, demanding the abolition of the celebration of October 12th as Columbus Day, "since this celebration emphasizes the beginning of the colonial trauma of the nation."

In the March 1965 issue of *Izkalotl* we find an important self-defense gesture: this is a petition to the President asking "for implementation of justice in the case of the assassination of the descendant of Cauhtemoc on the thirty-seventh kilometer from the village Santa Anita." A photograph of this descendant, a young man, accompanies this petition.

In the July 1965 issue of *Izkalotl,* there is, again, a bitter article condemning the neglect of police who had not yet identified the murderers of the young descendant of Cauhtémoc, though one year had gone by from the date of his assassination.

Such notes do remind, certainly, the members of the Movement of the continuity of the Nahuas' traumatic history, and mobilize them for further action. And they do remind Mexican society that this continuity is not forgotten.

In the area of international relations, *Izkalotl* has issued a number of proclamations, protests and political editorials described already in the chapter on ideology. Those international pronouncements can be divided into (1) those asserting the continental scope of the Movement's activities: the presence of the Movement's ambassadors and sympathizers throughout America: (2) those stressing sisterhood with other American republics liberated from Spanish rule but not yet culturally liberated from European influences; and (3) defensive pronouncements rejecting all sorts of foreign influences, mainly those of the United States but also those "of Europe and particularly Russia" with "its communism so foreign to aboriginal American thought." We also find in *Izkalotl* some specific protests, for instance, "energetic protests against drafting of Mexicans living in the United States to the army to fight in Vietnam" (*Izkalotl*, June 1967) or the article commenting on the pronouncement of the United States Presidents Eisenhower and Kennedy, that the U. S. Government does not have any territorial ambitions and intentions to dominate any nation. "But we Mexicans (*Izkalotl*, November/December 1960) in order to believe this, would have to receive first our territories taken from us by the United States during the war of 1847."

6. Their Identities: Lost and Regained

The term "Indian" is taboo among the members of the Movement of Reappearance of Anauak. This is a term mistakenly given by Europeans to American natives and perpetuated by Spaniards. It is a derogatory label imposed by enemies, which today symbolizes the natives' defeat, their enslavement, confusion, and hopelessness. I was warned not to ever use the term "Indian" in my writings, and to adopt the term "native Americans" instead. They themselves, however, use this clumsy term very rarely. They rather refer to themselves as "Nahuas," "Aztecs," "Mexicans," and sometimes, "Anauakians," inhabitants of Anauak.

When they speak of themselves as "Nahuas" they identify, mainly, as the descendants of the ancient Nahuas, inhabitants of the lands "extending from Nicaragua to the northern boundaries of today's State of California." They claim that Nahuas "were born in America, *Ixachilan* (in Nahuatl "Immensity")—they did not come from other continents, as Europeans present it."[37] Their culture is "auto-didactic," that is, they created it themselves, without any foreign influences.[38]

While referring to themselves as "Nahuas," they emphasize "the cultural significance of ancient Nahuas in America and in the World." While referring to themselves as "Aztecs," a less often used, and it seems, a still more prestigious identification, they emphasize their more immediate ancestors who "inspired by their forefathers' mandates, after a long-lasting march (two to eight hundred years) from the North, had founded Mexico-Tenochtitlan, and in less than two centuries, built the most powerful, benevolent, ingenious state: Confederation of Anauak."[39]

Identifying themselves as "Mexicans," the Movement's members are involved in a curious ambiguity, since to be a "Mexican" may mean (1) to be culturally Nahua and politically Aztec (i.e. *Mexica* or *Mexicano*), and (2) to be a modern Mexican of Mexican nationality and Mexican citizenship.

One of the most important goals of the Movement is to return to Mexican people their lost identity, and this lost identity can be best restored through their recruitment to the Movement. "Spanish domination," writes the late leader of the Movement, "deprived the Mexican of his own concepts, imposed its concepts, brainwashed him, and thus created in him an inferiority complex. In other words, Spanish domination robbed the Mexican of animistic and spiritual concepts, which every human being needs to progress."[40]

Even the "pure Mexicans" (and it is not clear to me whether the leaders of the Movement consider as "pure Mexicans" only the "racially" pure Aztecs, or whether they include in this category all those natives who did not mix with Spaniards), even those "pure Mexicans," though "not brainwashed, as have been others," have been, apparently reduced to passivity, to "patienhood," as Erik H. Erikson would put it.[41]

"The part of our population which did not cross with Spanish invaders," writes the late leader of the Movement, Rodolfo Nieva, "i.e. natives, remained outside of Hispanic-European influence, while this part of the population which crossed with invaders, has been maintaining Hispanic-European culture." The first ones have been maintaining a passive attitude, while the others have developed inferiority complexes due to their double personality, since they have been racially Mexicans and mentally Europeans.

This state of affairs is most responsible for the fact that the country remains so backward, underdeveloped and corrupt.''[42] Similar ideas are expressed in many "Proclamations to Mexicans," issued by the late leader of the Movement.

> Mexicans . . . you are a hybrid people, incapable of creating . . . You have been copying and imitating the people of white races in order to survive . . . You ignore your origins, you do not know from where you came . . . You do not know your mission in life, you do not even know whether you have any mission to accomplish. . . .
>
> You do not know what you want and where you go. You lack culture and national ideals, i.e. you lack those essential concepts which every human being, every country needs to progress toward the greatness. And besides:
>
> You are shy, fearful, because you are not sure of yourself. You lack confidence in your own faculties.
>
> You are, besides, conformist, resigned, and apathetic since you lack those moral stimuli which are provided by aspirations and ideals.
>
> This is why your character is weak, why you are not firm and constant. You underestimate yourself and overestimate everything foreign. You are individualist, not interested either in the fate of other Mexicans or in that of your country.
>
> And you are individualist. It bothers you when another Mexican succeeds and this is why you criticize him without pity until he is destroyed.
>
> To summarize: since the Spanish invasion you have been vegetating, not living![43]

The constructive part of this Proclamation advocates regaining lost identity through relearning of native culture, and the Reappearance of Anauak is presented—in a typically ambiguous way—as the only way of saving the Mexican Republic.

> Listen to me, Mexicans! (we read at the end of this Proclamation). According to the Destiny of our Nahuatl Race, Destiny which you ignore, you are supposed to go ahead and perfect yourself, since the Mexican Race should be again strong and powerful.
>
> The moment came in which you, Mexicans, should realize the mandates of your glorious ancestors.
>
> Wake up and go ahead!
>
> Get rid of the prejudices and complexes imposed by Spanish domination, which keep you in this deplorable state in which you live!

> Reconstruct your personality of a Mexican, with Mexican concepts and ideas which would make of your fatherland one of the first countries in the world!

Reconstruction of the lost identity has been attempted through all means at the disposal of the Movement, with the help of traditional religious and scientific legitimations, and through appeals to modern scientific, moral and economic arguments. It has been accomplished with the help of indoctrinating lectures, courses of Nahuatl, through organization of *calpullis* and Nahua ceremonies held on various occasions.

To what extent have the leaders, the members and the new converts to the Movement acquired the new proposed identifications? To what extent have they discarded the old ones? And what are the mechanisms of such changes?

Those are questions for the autobiographers of the Movement, for its historians and social scientists, who would read those autobiographies or be able to interview the members of the Movement. On the basis of my data I can only speculate a little about the complexities of such identifications.

It seems to me that the adherents of such ambitious, utopian movements, which have a large scope (continental, intercontinental or universal) and have no monastic, exclusive character but are rather missionary, open, staying "within the world," do have something in common. It seems that the members of such movements, in order to achieve at least some of their objectives, and for their own mental health, as well, have to live carefully balanced "double-lives," and that the understanding of this nonhypocritical duplicity is essential, indeed, for an understanding of their identifications. In order to convert others who still accept the "old reality" they have to move easily within this "old reality," to share at least in some of the activities and values of the people whom they plan to convert. And since their "new reality" does not yet exist, they do rely for their livelihood on the old one. In order to survive and to be able to structure their Movement they have to have rather deep roots in the world they criticize, condemn and reject. And this is, certainly, the case of those neo-Nahua intellectuals.

In spite of its civilizatory character, ancient Nahua culture was open to the influences of other cultures. It was particularly syncretic in the area of religion, adding new symbols and new deities from people with whom they came into contact, from friends and even enemies. For centuries the invaded natives of Mexico have practiced mixtures of Catholicism with their own religions, without seeing anything strange or wrong with such a syncretism. Uneducated members co-opted to the Movement feel, very likely, the same way about being Mexicans (in a modern sense of this word) as about being Nahuas, and most of them have been recruited from among Nahuatl-speaking groups or the populations of Nahua origin anyway. Though, according to the Movement's plans, Catholicism is to disappear from the future Confederation of Anauak, Catholic beliefs and rituals are never condemned by the Movement. But there is an attempt instead to make the revived Nahua beliefs and rituals more relevant and more attractive.

Do those neo-Nahua intellectuals *really believe* in what they profess, I have often asked myself. I saw them exalted by their ceremonies and heard deep conviction in their voices when they tried to convey to potential members their utopian ideas—"unrealizable," as I reflected, "within the modern world." On a few occasions I even expressed to ingeniero X my profound doubts in regard to such plans as the elimination of Spanish as a national language and reintroduction of Nahuatl, and in regard to the peaceful remaking of Mexican capitalism into *calpulli*-type communalism.

But those modern Mexican lawyers, doctors, engineers, scholars, do believe, it seems, in what they profess. He gave me examples of many historical and more contemporary social movements with even more utopian ideologies, and he reminded me of the Movement's theory of "cosmic cataclysm" which would help, "in a still unknown way," in the revival of the modernized Confederation of Anauak.

CONCLUSIONS

1. Native Mexican Intellectuals and Indianists

History judges us not in terms of our private behavior, our intentions and dreams but in terms of those intentions and dreams that get expressed in writing and action. Today, in the era of mass media, this has to be a well-advertised, attention-attracting writing, and spectacular, well-publicized action.

No social movement can survive today without some type of publicity. The "Realist" Indian intellectuals specialize in short, clearly formulated statements, demanding social justice for Indian masses. They inject such statements into all sorts of public meetings dealing directly or indirectly with Indian problems.

"Utopians" from the Movement of Reappearance of Anauak publicize their presence in Mexico through infrequent but very well-staged Aztec ceremonies held on the streets of Mexico City, silent and sacred in deliberate contrast to the secular and noisy Mexican national celebrations. And they have been asserting their presence through spectacular, highly symbolic "suppers" to which members of the press, selected Mexican intellectuals and foreign diplomats are invited.

Indian "Realists," whatever their private dreams and nostalgia, publically emphasize their minimalistic but still tremendously difficult program of the incorporation of Indians as equals into the national society, under the leadership of educated natives. Their political platform has been that of the restoration of social justice for the most unjustly treated segment of the Mexican society. Whatever their individual political affiliations (and some of them are

103

members of PPS, *Partido Popular Socialista*, advocating some sort of social democracy) officially they strongly endorse the government's national ideology, rooted in the Mexican Revolution. This ideology, though, according to them, already greatly distorted, has still been to some extent alive in PRI, the party in power.

The "Realists' " slogan, printed on the first page of their magazine, *Cuadernos del AMPII*, "To Mexicanize Indians - not to Indianize Mexico" expresses well their fundamental agreement with the Mexican government's *Indianist* policies. From the historical viewpoint, however, such an agreement means some type of reconciliation with the consequences of the Spanish invasion. Though critical and resentful of the mestizo conception of Mexico, as formulated during the Mexican Independence, and confirmed by the Mexican Revolution, the "Realists" have accepted "the irreversible fact" that Mexico is to remain an Indian-Spanish, mestizo country of "two bloods and two traditions," a country of "creative marginality."

Incorporation of Indians into national society, they have argued, has to be accomplished with minimal suffering, maximum self-determination, and therefore under the leadership of educated Indians themselves since nobody else can fully understand and is able to gain the confidence of Indian masses. If implemented on a large-scale such a policy would incorporate most Indians as equals into Mexican society, and leave others as non-deprived rural ethnic groups, accepted as such, largely self-sufficient but given equal opportunity to participate in the national society, and helped by this society in case of need.

Indianists (*Indigenistas*) and Indianism (*Indigenismo*) may be defined in two ways. If we define Indianism as "sympathetic awareness of the Indian"[1] we may argue that Indianism in a small but significant way existed already in the earliest times of Spanish occupation. Truly great and courageous Indianists can be found among Spanish monks, such as Las Casas or Vasco de Quiroga, who openly denounced colonial policies toward Indians and tried to help natives in a variety of ways, often at the cost of great personal risks and sacrifices. Throughout all periods of the Colony there existed some Indianists and some Indianism in this sense of the word.

The Movement of Independence had a strong Indianist ideology in this sense, as well as in its emphasis on (a) acceptance of the fusion of the two races as the essence of Mexican personality, (b) in the faith in the educability of the, apparently, "inferior" Indian, (c) in the adoption of a fundamental liberal view of race.[2] Even during the period of the dictatorship of Porfirio Diáz—long and, probably, the

most difficult period for Mexican natives since the War of Independence,[3] there were some outspoken Indianists in Mexico, arguing
for Indian rights. Indianism, however, "came into full flower" only
two decades after the Mexican Revolution, around 1930.[4]

If we accept a more operational definition of "Indianism" as an
institutionalized way of implementing governmental policies toward
Indians, we may then argue that Indianism started in Mexico in 1948
only when the INI, *Instituto Nacional Indigenista* (National Indianist
Institute) was created.

We may also see Indianism as a rather loose social movement, with
its roots in the Colony, a movement rather silent in some, but outspoken
in other periods of Mexican history, a movement with a very heterogeneous membership and with shifting ideologies. We may even go
so far ás a to argue that this movement was transformed, incorporated
or "swallowed" by the government, and after this had happened, it
lost its previous spontaneous pro-Indian character, and became an
arm of government designed "to solve the Indian problem." "Our
goal," writes the first director of INI (*Instituto Nacional Indigenista*),
great Mexican archeologist, Alfonso Caso, "is to accelerate the changes
which are otherwise inevitable and which will lead to transformation
of the Indian community into Mexican peasant community."[5]

There exist in contemporary Mexico, it seems, at least four types
of Indianists:

(1) Those who were a part of the Indianist movement before the
INI was created and joined the Institute as its employees but never
lost their social-movement mentality of dedicated idealistic and independent Indianists.

(2) Those who joined the INI as its employees but were never
Indianists in the previous sense of the word. They only implement
the governmental policies toward natives, without questioning or
evaluating them independently in terms of the welfare of natives
themselves.

(3) Those whom I called "New Indianists" and who refer to themselves as "critical anthropologists."[6] Their position is briefly formulated in a university magazine *Comunidad*.[7] Their main targets are
"Indianist bureaucrats and anthropologists connected with Indianism." They accuse them of performing "genocide" and "ethnocide" on
Indians. They criticize the Indianist policy of the Mexican government, this policy consisting, according to them, of attempts to create
a "homogeneous society" and "national character" without taking
into consideration the cultural heterogeneity of the country. Such a

policy implies, according to them, "destruction of the distinct local structures and conversion of the Indian into Mexican citizen." They further emphasize that "such a destruction is being justified by the ideal of the Mexican Revolution and at the same time considered an irreversible historical process." Instead of changing Indians, they advocate, the social structure of Mexico should be changed in such a way that cultural and social diversity would be encouraged. They advocate some sort of cultural pluralism instead of national homogeneity. "In Mexico," they claim (and they mean "in a future, better Mexico"), "Indians will disappear but different cultures or rather distinct societies will persist."

(4) There are, finally, those Indianists in Mexico who never joined INI and either individually or through the recently emerging New Indianists' movement, have been trying to help natives in various ways. They do not belong to any specific group, and their Indianistic efforts, their individualistic style of writing and action, are somewhat similar to those of the earliest colonial Indianists.

There are, naturally, misunderstandings, hidden and open conflicts among members of those four categories of Indianists. And there exist hidden and open conflicts between natives of various types and Indianists of various faiths as well.

So far there have been relatively few natives in Mexican Indianist movements and in Mexican National Indianist Institute (INI), though there have been recently some attempts on the part of the current President of Mexico, Luis Echaverriá, to recruit educated natives into all those national institutions which are concerned with Indian affairs. In the INI itself there are several Mexican natives high up in the Institute's bureaucracy.

"Utopians" from the Movement of Reappearance of Anauak with their nonviolent, revisionary but maximalistic ideology and program of restoration of the Confederation of Anauak, do not accept, of course, either the policy of "incorporation of Indians into Mexican society," advocated by INI, or the Indians' endorsed version of the same program, promoted by the "Realist" professionals and intellectuals from AMPII. They disregard, however, rather than reject the "Realists'" ideology and activities. They also disregard the ideology of "critical anthropologists" and their program.

Their cultural reconstruction activity, establishing new *calpullis*, doing intensive research, publications, and keeping the movement intensely alive, absorb them completely. They continue to build their "parallel society," without being greatly involved either in attempts at establishment of contacts with Indianists or in critiques of their platform. Their polemics are rather historical and philosophical than political, and their built-in ambiguity in the use of the terms "Mexico" and "Mexican," prevents them, probably, from specific polemical attacks.

I heard, however, that there were some "summit conversations" between the leaders of the "Realists" and leaders of "Utopians." Those conversations, apparently, did not yield any results because of the "Realists'" opinion that "those people from the Academy of Nahuatl Language do not recognize all Indian groups as equal, accepting as equals only those who are racially pure, like Tarahumaras or Yaquis"[8] and that "they advocate the idea of the Confederation of Anauak under the leadership of Aztecs only . . . "

2. Tomorrow

There are few, if any, postcolonial societies today in which a national culture has solidified and stabilized. Postcolonial societies, both old and new, are still building their national cultures, trying to develop a sense of unity and belongingness which would allow their people to relax intellectually, morally, emotionally, to forget, in the name of such commitments to a national culture, about universal human problems.

For some time, at least for a century, we have been living in an era of a scarcity of attractive universalistic ideologies either of a religious or of a secular character. And only such ideologies could stimulate the rise of non-nationalistic societies, so much more suitable for our modern, culturally heterogeneous world; societies built upon what Durkheim would call "organic solidarity,"[9] associational societies of loyal but differentiated citizens.

Most of the national ideologies which emerged in the twentieth century and keep emerging in the new post-colonial societies are of a narrow, nationalistic character, and are usually incongruent with the outlook on life[10] imposed or forced upon decolonized natives by occidentalized elites.

Though the influence of the French Revolution upon the Mexican War of Independence (1810) is strongly stressed in the Mexican literature of this era. I doubt whether the French revolutionary ideals of equality and justice did, really, penetrate the large strata of that early nineteenth century Mexican society, a society composed of strongly subordinated and heterogeneous native groups, Spanish creoles, and mestizos, just acquiring their new consciousness.

Being a spontaneous, nonintellectual, diffused movement of lower, less gratified, more amesticized (of "mixed blood") and worse "connected" colonizers, the Mexican Movement of Independence, could not possibly have been inspired as a whole by the ideals of the French Revolution. It was probably inspired by the more recent and both geographically and socially closer Revolution of the neighboring colonial society, which culminated in the creation of the United States of America.

This was, probably, the only model really available to those implementors of the Mexican Independence who had to name and organize their new decolonized society.

But even this geographically close model was far from being suitable for Mexico. The background of the natives was very different in the two countries and their treatment by the Spanish invaders varied greatly from their treatment by Anglo-Saxon invaders.

The Social origins of the Spanish invaders, their cultural aspirations and their political goals were also very different from those of the Anglo-Saxons. Eager to finish with "savages" and start working independently on their own pieces of land, the Anglo-Saxons killed as many natives as possible, pushing the survivors far away from their sight so they could not give "bad examples" of "laziness and lack of discipline" to hard working pioneer farmers. The same attitude toward the natives continued after the Independence from England was won. The country was named the "United States of America." No attempt was made to name it after some of the native tribes, and there was no idealization at that time of those nonagrarian, non-Christian, and therefore "not quite human Indian savages."

The Spanish invaders brought very different cultural models to Mexico: these were not models of laboring farmers, but of land-owning *bon-vivants*, adventurers, fascinated with the world around them. After the initial massacres of the Invasion they started to baptize the "pagan natives," marrying their women and resettling the invaded populations in such a way that they could control them and exploit their labor as well as possible. And at the same time they were fascinated with the invaded country, her history and her "Indians." The city built on the ruins of destroyed Tenochtitlan could certainly have been named "New Madrid" or "New Toledo," or named after Cortés or after Columbus, but it was called "Ciudad de Mexico," the most impressive from among the invaded inhabitants (*Mexica*, i.e. Aztecs) being honored at least in this way. For the same reason, as well as for ideological reasons, (recognition of the reality and principle of "two bloods and two traditions: Indian and Spanish") the name "Mexico" was given to the decolonized New Spain, which could have been called differently . . . for instance, "United States of Middle America."

Instead of being subordinated, the natives of Independent Mexico were to be integrated, to become a functioning part of this new mestizo country. The new national culture and the new national character were supposed to be made out of the integrated Spanish-Indian characteristics, the formula which has been repeated throughout all stages of Mexican history, and which is still strong today, but which did not ever really work. Neither national culture nor national character have been built so far in Mexico.[11] It was, probably, altogether impossible to create a homogeneous national culture out of such highly heterogeneous "material" without the help of mass media. After all, the subculture of the colonizers themselves was highly differentiated and this differentiation was transformed into a still more complex social and cultural differentiation during the times of the Colony. The so-called "Indians," though treated as an undifferentiated mass by the invaders, consisted of more than two hundred various groups, ranging from those whose ancestors developed high civilizations to simple nomadic tribes. If some other models were available at that time, or if the makers of Mexico had been less ignorant of the variety of strictly native models, maybe a very different and happier Mexico would have been built out of the decolonized New Spain.

But this did not happen, and like other decolonized Latin American countries, Mexico became politically organized as a democratic Republic with a highly individualized capitalistic economic structure.

It is my contention that the Mexican "presidential monarchy," with its strong governmental controls, has saved Mexico from even greater misfortunes,[12] which would probably have resulted from the more literal attempts at implementation of twentieth century style laissez faire democratic capitalism.

Such social movements as these two could not have flourished in the country without some type of tolerance, and there must be a great deal of such tolerance in Mexico, if a movement promoting such a complete remaking of the socio-political structure of Mexico as does the Movement of Reappearance of Anauak is allowed to function.

If nationalism, self-assured and fanatic—such as had developed in some European countries[13]—had developed in Mexico, the Mexican one-party-directed democracy could have become much more suppressive than it is of the citizens' freedoms.[14] But such nationalism has never, so far, developed. Nationalistic conceptions have been, fortunately, never philosophically consistent and politically institutionalized in Mexico. Too interested in everything around them, too intelligent and inquiring (*inquietos*), Mexicans have been permanently dissatisfied, constantly searching for new paths, new solutions, new models.

Large scale decolonization of Asia and Africa, revindication of native cultures throughout the world, creation of the United Nations, awareness of the so-called "Third World" and the spectacular social and political failures of major nationalistic powers all have had tremendous impact not only on Mexican intellectuals but also, due to the mass media, on larger strata of the Mexican population. Scholars, writers, and politicans residing in Mexico, most but not all Mexicans, started reflecting on alternatives for Latin America in general and for Mexico in particular. They generally approve the already traditional Mexican political style of neutral vacillation between great powers. They are critical of both Soviet-type communism, and U. S.-type capitalism. They inquire into both right-and left-wing ideologies and structures, in order to "improve," "save" or "solve" in order to be economically and culturally independent and in order not to succumb to any brand of real dictatorship.

The awareness of a greater and greater discrepancy between the elites and masses, (contrary to the ideology of the Mexican Revolution), have produced such definition of Mexican economy as being in the era of "growth without development"[15] and there has been much reflection in all Indianist milieux about the place of native populations within the modern world.

As seen against this background the two social movements described in this book voice and symbolize—each in a different way—the key national Mexican problems which torment this imperfect but very much alive and very idealistic Republic.

The "Realist" Indian intellectuals from AMPII remind Mexico of its commitments to social justice for native populations, so idealized in Mexican revolutionary ideology, and so forgotten half a century after the Mexican Revolution.

The "Utopian" intellectuals from the Movement of Reappearance of Anauak have dramatically defined for Mexico (what neither the Movement of Independence nor the Revolution had ever clearly defined)—the meaning of the native past.

Though neither program has a chance of being accepted today by the large strata of population, both movements are allowed to function, to assemble, protest, promote, publish and in a small way they both concretely influence contemporary Mexican reality.

Will they have a larger impact in the future?

I do not see much chance of all Indianist positions being taken over in the near future by educated Indians, as the members of AMPII advocate. There would simply not be enough educated Indians. To be an "Indian" one has to be not only of native origin but also to practice some of the native culture and to identify as "Indian," which is made difficult for those with higher education.

The introduction of Nahuatl as a national language, revival of Nahua philosophy and religion as a basis of national life, and acceptance of the large-scale communal *calpulli* economic structure is even less likely to occur, unless, of course, some cosmic disaster will "help" or even necessitate this type of restructuring.

But, perhaps, the successes of social movements should not be assessed in terms of the achievement of their avowed objectives as very few, indeed, do achieve them. Nevertheless, these movements often have a profound impact on the societies within which they function. They influence them in the way none of the official institutions are able to, despite the whole governmental apparatus at their disposal.

The political sect of St-Simonism (started after the death of St-Simon in 1825) was much smaller and more extravagant than the Movement of Reappearance of Anauak, and still had a great impact not only on France, but on all intellectual Europe.[26] This political sect with its handful of members, monastery, "Pope," and New "Bible of Technology," though not even lasting for the lifetime of its members, truly remade the European centuries-old attitudes toward science and social organization. It greatly secularized Europe and it made scientific planning both acceptable and respectable.[17]

In order to accelerate such ("inevitable," as one would tend to think today) secularization of society, St-Simonists had to make a dramatic appearance, with monastery, pope, monastic robes. "Realist" intellectuals from AMPII make their dramatic appearances during Mexican congresses and symposiums at which the Indian problems are discussed directly or even indirectly. Intellectuals from the "Utopian" Movement of the Reappearance of Anauak hold their Nahua ceremonies in the midst of the modern Mexico City.

Maybe in our era of mass media and concerns with national visibility it takes that much or even more to have our ideas on the importance of social justice for deprived people, and of their cultural rights, to be heard and taken into account.

NOTES

1. Terminology

Mexico, as other Republics on the American continent, is seen in this book as a postcolonial country established through European invasion of native American lands and the subsequent separation of the victorious colonizers from their European fatherlands.

To various degrees the European colonizers mixed genetically and culturally with the peoples of the invaded nations. To various degrees they also incorporated native cultural themes into their national ideologies. In a number of ways they supplemented their colonial and postcolonial European populations with more recent immigrants from a wide spectrum of European countries. The methods of extermination, exploitation, and patronisation adopted toward the invaded populations were not consistent from one country to another and from one historical period to another. Though Mexico not only had its "War of Independence" but also a large-scale popular "Revolution," both movements are seen in this book as organized by or in the interest of the European invaders and their culturally related European descendants.

For this reason I contemplated the idea of using, throughout this book, the names of those two great liberating movements in quotation marks, as I did above. I decided, however, against it since such quotation marks could have offended many Mexicans whom I highly respect and admire. Even such extreme nativists as the "Utopians" described in this book do not use the terms "War of Independence" and "Revolution" in quotation marks. Although not their own liberation

112

movements, those two great uprisings did liberate them to some extent —they claim.

I used the terms "natives" or "aboriginals" throughout this book to refer to both ancient indigenous Mexican populations and those of their descendants who preserved either their identification with their respective aboriginal groups or some of the cultural traits of those groups, such as language, beliefs, and style of life. As I had much opportunity to verify personally,[1] many natives identify themselves as Mazahuas, Otomies, Purépechas, Mexicas, Tzeltales, etc., and consider the term "Indian," applied to them by the non-native population, as false and derogatory.

The term "Indian" is used, however, in this book to refer to those natives who were reduced to being Indians, and accepted this label as their fate. They became Indians as a consequence of the long process of deculturation and subordination, both in the colonial and postcolonial eras.

Some of the Mexican natives with higher education, as it was shown in this book, though seen as "Mexicans" by the non-native Mexican population, deliberately identify themselves as "Indians" in order to assert their solidarity with those Mexican natives who were reduced to "Indianhood." In Mexico (unlike the United States) it is the culture, language, style of life and identity, rather than skin color, which distinguishes "Indian" from "non-Indian." An educated native is automatically, and sometimes against his desire, considered to be "Mexican."

Mexicans—inhabitants of Mexico who live according to modified Spanish culture—are often called by anthropologists and sociologists "mestizos," the term referring to either genetic or both genetic and cultural hybridization. Mexicans, however, never refer to themselves this way, and are rarely called mestizos by other native and non-native inhabitants of this country. The term "mestizo," though sometimes used, was generally avoided in this book. Consistent use of this term, could, indeed, suggest the paradoxical conclusion that Mexico is a country without Mexicans. The term "Mexican" was used here for all of those who identified themselves as Mexicans, and practiced some of the Mexican culture, independently of their origins and their citizenship. There would be some natives among Mexicans understood in this way, and some recent European immigrants as well.

Whatever their good will and determination about not hurting those about whom they write, social scientists involved in a study of contemporary people end by hurting some of them anyway. If the people whom we interviewed use, for example, contradictory terminology, and if there is no possibility of finding or inventing neutral terms with which they would all agree, the investigator is bound to offend some of them and to lose their respect and friendship. This is a great risk, of course, and one sometimes wonders whether our changing hypotheses about social reality make up for such damaging losses.

I used two criteria in the selection of controversial terms throughout this book: 1) I tried to select a term which, according to my best knowledge, would give the most truthful description of the investigated reality; 2) where it was not possible to make a judgement on such empirical truthfulness, I selected a term which would hurt the least vulnerable from among my interviewees. In case of the term "Confederation of Anauak," which I have been using throughout this book instead of the well-established and more respectable term "Aztec Empire," I have to admit that I was truly convinced by my "Utopian" interviewees from the "Movement of Reappearance of Anauak" that the latter term was ethnocentric, while the former one corresponded better to the Mexican precolonial reality, and was more neutral. But I did not adopt the term "pre-Cauhtémocian" (before the time of Cauhtémoc) which my interviewees from this Movement asked me to use instead of the traditional "precolonial," since I do not see anything wrong with such terms as "precolonial" or "preindustrial." If they are used as descriptive historical terms—as they are in this book —they, certainly, do not presuppose any evolutionary theory according to which colonial or industrial "stages" were to succeed the precolonial or preindustrial "stages of development." On the other hand, I prefer to avoid such terms as "pre-Colombian" or "pre-Cauhtémocian" not only because of the value judgements attached to the roles of those historical figures, but because of my sociological rather than historical orientation. If Cauhtémoc had created a major social movement or introduced major legislation, I would write without hesitation about a "Cauhtémocian era" and "pre-Cauhtémocian era."

2. Methodology and Ethics

The data of famous social science classics consist usually either of historical accounts or their own casual observations and interviewing. Sometimes they consist of such documents as census or newspaper accounts.

Those great men did not have tape recorders and computers at their disposal but were able to control far better than we do their main instruments of investigation, their well-trained, disciplined minds.

Their ability to observe their environment, and draw inferences from it, their use of historical and cross-cultural analogies, their reliance on enlightened common sense, and their ability to communicate their knowledge to educated (though not specialized) readers can be envied by many of us. Their studies were of suggestive rather than verifying character. Without being called "consultants," they acted as high level consultants to their educated contemporaries, some of them men of power, most men of intellect, which in those times implied at least a latent social power.

Though I was trained in a rather rigid empirical sociology of a sophisticated quantitative type, I never practice this type of sociology in my research. Using the much less rigid research style of social anthropologists, and inspired by the classics of social sciences, I always have been acutely aware, however, of the tentativeness of such findings, in which correct sampling and other controls customary to more scientific research can seldom be used. I often tell my sociology students that, in fact, most research on significant social issues is done in the "waiting room of science," and that keeping this "waiting room" well-illuminated and clean is no less important than taking care of "science parlors."

Two social movements organized by Mexican natives with higher education are described and compared in this book. Those comparisons are made in spite of the fact that data on one movement differ greatly from the data on another. Whatever our wishful thinking it is hard in social sciences to collect exactly comparable data anyway, unless, of course, we decide to study something relatively simple and trivial rather than complex and significant. The members of one movement, whom I named "Realists," were willing to be interviewed and I had a chance to talk with them for long hours and sometimes on several occasions. The members of the other movement, whom I called "Utopians" did not want to be interviewed but provided me with their publications and invited me to several lectures and ceremonies during which I was able to get acquainted with some of the movement's leaders and their followers, and to observe many more.

In both cases, I explained clearly the purpose of my research and showed my informants the tentative plan of my book. I assured them of my intention to be as discrete as possible in the presentation of the data and about strict personal anonymity. Such assurances come often as an unpleasant surprise to various interviewees, who would prefer their names to be known, and one has to argue sometimes very hard to persuade them that the anonymity is in their best interest.

When I explained to my informants that my study would be to some extent comparative, that I would occasionally try to compare native Mexican intellectuals to other intellectuals from colonial, postcolonial and noncolonial societies, I encountered strong opposition from a few persons in both social movements. From their specific postcolonial perspective, comparison to others (and particularly to intellectuals from European societies) meant criticism, assertion of superiority, imposition—even an attempt to overshadow the hardships which Mexican natives have been experiencing for several centuries. I hope, however, that I genuinely managed to persuade them that my comparisons were not intended to be aggressive and derogatory and that without some comparative perspective this type of sociological investigation would lose much of its value.

Most accounts of social movements and particularly those organized by educated people come from participants or escapees from those movements, and have been analyzed only *post factum* by social scientists. Studies of social movements done through participant observation have usually been done among non-educated people from lower social strata, who either allowed sympathetic social scientists into their social movements with the hope of some concrete gains, or were "inflitrated" by them under some well-planned pretext.

The difficulties of making a completely honest study of a social movement in general, and even more so of a social movement organized by educated people, are tremendous. The educated interviewees, as a rule, try to become co-researchers and co-authors of the investigator, and the investigator may easily be converted to their well-argued points of view, thus losing the objectivity and detachment so necessary in any research. And if some of our interviewees are social scientists themselves, then the situation becomes often so difficult that the very existence of empirical social science has to be questioned. Have we or have we not a moral right to study objectively those with whose ideas we may strongly disagree and who expect our sympathetic loyalty or even our active support? And if we become converted to a controversial viewpoint advanced by a given social movement, do we still have a moral right to claim our scholarly objectivity while describing this movement?

The studies of the two social movements presented in this book were done to a small extent through participant-observation. The study of "Realists" is mainly based on long and usually repeated interviews with thirteen native Mexican professionals selected from among the members of their association. No formal sampling procedure was used, however, in selecting my interviewees. Such formal sampling was not attempted mainly because of the great importance I attached to good rapport with my interviewees. I interviewed only those who really wanted to be interviewed. My study of this movement is thus based on a "self-selected sample"—a horrible sociological sin for which I do not apologize but on which I do want to comment a little more. In order to investigate the Indian "Realists" more scientifically, I should have reached first of all not only those who identified as "Indians" but those members of the Movement who stopped identifying as "Indians," and "dissolved" into Mexican society as well. It was relatively easy to get the addresses of those "drop-outs" from the Movement; I decided, however, not to interview them. I just did not want to force them to review with me their certainly difficult decisions. I did not want to revive their hesitations. It is so hard—I reflected—to help people through our research, and so easy to damage them.

The study of the "Utopians" is mainly based on an analysis of all the issues of their monthly magazine *Izkalotl* which has been published in Mexico City for over fifteen years, on the basis of several publications by the Movement's members, and some polemics with this Movement found in the Mexican press. Those data were supplemented with several personal and numerous telephone conversations with one of the Movement's leaders and with participation in several lectures and ceremonies organized by the Movement.

As always, but in this case to an even greater extent, I had many doubts on how to conduct my research, about what to write and about what not to write in order to be completely fair toward all those persons who so generously gave me their time and who showed me such great confidence. My doubts were particularly strong in case of the "Utopians" who did not want to be interviewed but nevertheless invited me to their lecures and ceremonies, and conversed with me on those occasions. Since those invitations came at the end of my research, I was never clear whether I was invited there as a sociologist or as their friend, and consequently I have been very hesitant about using the data gathered during those visits in this book.

There is one ethical rule which I understood for the first time fully on the occasion of this particular research. One does not have the right, I think, to write in any sociological book, based on direct human contact, anything which the people in question would not like to convey themselves to their society or to the larger world. This criterion has to be used, naturally, according to the investigator's best judgement since it is impossible to disturb one's informants with hundreds of questions.

However discreet and efficient they may be, any techniques of eliciting data which the informants would not like to convey, and any analysis of the data received through direct human contact in terms of "latent functions" is, in my judgment, unfair toward the informants, to say the least.

The most important role for the sociologist working on this type of research is, I think, that of an impartial but sympathetic intellectual mediator between the people studied and their own society. This is not an easy role, and I would be very happy, indeed, if this book helped the native intellectuals from the two social movements even in the slightest way to continue their important dialogues with Mexican society, dialogues which they initiated so imaginatively and so courageously.

3. ENDNOTES
INTRODUCTION

1. In his book *Modern Nationalities* (Urbana: The University of Illinois Press, 1952), Florian Znaniecki writes about two types of literary culture societies: religious (based on sacred religious books) and national (based on secular books).

2. Eric Wofl, *Sons of the Shaking Earth* (Chicago: The University of Chicago Press, 1959).

3. The term "nationality" is used by Znaniecki *(op. cit.)* interchangeably with a longer term "national culture society." He warns the reader that "nationality" should not be confused with "nation-state," since there are many nationalities which never had (or lost) political independence.

4. The attempts and failures of national unification efforts in Mexico are well presented in a recently published book by Francisco Gonzalez Pineda and Antonio Delhumeau (Mexico City: *Lost Mexicanos Frente al Poder*, Instituto Mexicano de Estudios Políticos, A.C., Mexico City, 1973).

5. An excellent study of the social use of the "race" concept is that of Julien Pitt-Rivers "Race in Latin America: the Concept of 'Raza,' " *Archives Europeens de Sociologie*, Vol. 14, 1973.

6. Wm. Bruce Cameron, *Modern Social Movements* (New York: Random House, 1966), p. 7.

7. See the UNESCO position on such issues in *Cultural Rights as Human Rights*, Studies and Documents on Cultural Policies, No. 3, UNESCO, 1970.

8. Mrs. Hilda Obregon who was most kind and helpful during this research.

9. I am most grateful for all help given me by the members of the Instituto Indigenista Interamericano.

10. Called "Professor Barrios Ortega" throughout this book. He did not want to be formally interviewed but I was in frequent contact with him and he was an excellent informant.

11. Alicja Iwańska, *Purgatory and Utopia* (Cambridge, Mass.: Schenkman Publishing Co., 1971); *idem, Purgatorio y Utopia* (Mexico City: SepSetentas, 41, 1971).

12. J. K. Zawodny, *Death in the Forest: The Story of Katyń Forest Massacre* (Notre Dame, University of Notre Dame Press, 1962).

BACKGROUND

1. Alan Wells, *Picture Tube Imperalism* (Maryknoll, New York: Orbis Books, 1972), discusses the impact of U.S. television on Latin America.

2. David A. Branding, *Los Origenes del Nacionalismo Mexicano* (Mexico City: SepSetentas No. 82, 1973).

3. Octavio Paz, "Laberinto de Soledad," *Cuadernos Americanos*, Mexico 1950.

4. Eric Wolf, "The Virgen de Guadalupe," *Journal of American Folklore*, Vol. 71, 1958.

5. Frank Brandenburg, *The Making of Modern Mexico* (New York: Prentice Hall, 1970), and José Vasconcelos, *La Raza Cósmica* (Buenos Aires: Espasa Celpa, 1948).

6. Martin Staab, "Indigenism and Racism in Mexican Thought: 1857-1911," *Journal of Interamerican Studies*, October, 1959.

7. Gonzalo Aguirre Beltrán, *Regiones de Refugio*, Instituto Indigenista Interamericano, Ediciones Especiales, 46, Mexico, 1967.

8. Paz, *op. cit.*, p. 120.

9. Such crimes as the bloody purges within the Communist Party in 1938, pogroms of Jews, the 1939 pact with Hitler and subsequent invasion of Eastern Europe.

10. Paz, *op. cit.*

11. *Mi Libro de Quarto Año* (Mexico City: Comisión Nacional de los Libros de Texto Gratuitos, 1960).

PART I: REALISTS

1. Speaking to little children in Spanish, in order to help them with their future, was a rule in the little Mazahua village (where practically everybody was bilingual but where Mazahua only was spoken among adults and children) (Iwańska, *op. cit.*, 1971).

2. Lourdes Arizpe, *Indígenas en la Ciudad de México, El Caso de las "Marías"* (Mexico City: SepSetentas, 1975), on migration from one village of Mazahua tradition, to Mexico City. According to this data, collected by demographer Augustin Porras during the decade 1950-1960, as many as 25.4 percent of all women and 21.4 percent of the men emigrated permanently from this village.

3. Though infant mortality greatly decreased in Mexico during the last half century due to improvement of medical services, hygiene and diet, the situation in the areas inhabited by many natives had not yet caught up with this progress. The number of children in the families from which my interviewees came ranged from five to thirteen, the average number of children per family being thus 7.5. In order to find out about the life chances of those children, I asked everyone interviewed how many of his siblings survived until the present. Their answers suggest that only about one-third of the children born to rural native families in Mexico during the first half of the twentieth century had a chance of reaching adulthood.

4. This term is used by Stanislaw Andreski in his book *Parasitism and Subversion, The Case of Latin America* (New York: Schoken Books, 1966).

5. One of the interviewees described his native village as being divided today into four political parties, and "plagued" by protestant missionaries in addition to this.

6. The term coined under the presidency of Cárdenas who organized "Cultural Missions" in Mexico.

7. I heard that the same rumors were current in a Mazahua village where I conducted my research during the thirties, Iwańska, *op. cit.*, 1971.

8. I observed this obsession with details of empirical truth both among the Tzeltales of Chiapas and the Mazahuas of Central Mexico. Alicja Iwańska, "El Concepto del Indígena en dos Distintas Regiones de Mexico," *America Indígena*, Vol. 23, No. 4, October, 1963.

9. This term refers to a laissez faire type of economic growth, which in underdeveloped or developing nations creates often a high per capita income at the cost of a greater and greater economic and social gap between upper and lower social strata. This type of growth—argue those economists—creates painful and dangerous unrest rather than harmonious socioeconomic development.

10. Alicja Iwańska, "The Mexican Indian Image and Identity," *Journal of Inter-American Studies* Vol. 6, No. 4, 1964; and Iwańska *op. cit.*, 1970.

11. Iwańska, *op. cit.*, 1971.

PART II: UTOPIANS—YESTERDAY

1. Demetrio Sodi in his book, *La Literatura de los Mayas* (Mexico City: Editorial Joaquín Mortiz, 1964), explains why so little is known about Maya intellectuals.

2. According to Edward Shils, "The Intellectuals and the Powers" in Philip Rieff, ed., *On Intellectuals* (New York: Doubleday & Co., Inc., 1970), pp. 27-28, "There is in every society a minority of persons who, more than the ordinary run of their fellowmen, are inquiring and desirous of being in frequent communion with symbols which are more general than the immediate, concrete situation of everyday life and remote in their reference in both time and space. In this minority there is a need to externalize this quest in oral and written discourse, in poetic or plastic expression, in historical reminiscence or writing, in ritual performance and acts of worship."

3. The key sources on earlier Nahaua and Aztec intellectuals used in this study are: Jacque Soustelle, *La Vie Cotidienne des Aztèques* (Paris: Librairie Hachette, 1955); Miguel Leon Portilla, *La Filosofía Nahuatl*, (Mexico City: UNAM, 1959); *Visión de los Vencidos* (Mexico City: UNAM, 1961); and *idem*, *Aztec Thought and Culture (A Study of the Ancient Nahuatl Mind)* (Norman, Okl., University of Oklahoma Press, 1963).

4. Hernán Cortés, *Cartas de Relaciones de la Conquista* (Mexico City: Editorial Porrua, 1960). Bernal Diáz de Castillo, *Historia Verdadera de la Conquista de la Nueva España* (Mexico City: Editorial Porrua, 1960).

5. A good example of such an outstanding intellectual, capable of detachment, a critical attitude toward his society and great social commitment, is Nezahualcoyotl (1402—1472), king of Texcoco, great Nahua ruler, architect and poet.

6. Portilla, *op. cit.*, 1963, p. 10.

7. This version of the communication between Cortés and Montezuma is based on a variety of sources (including some articles in *Izkalotl*). This is my own interpretation of those events, which may be, naturally, mistaken, but which seems to me to be most convincing.

8. Portilla, *op. cit.*, 1961, from XIII, *Relacion de Alvar Ixtlilxochitl*, p. 136.

PART II: UTOPIANS—TODAY

1. Wells, *op. cit.*

2. I conducted research in Mexico for over a decade studying village Indians and mestizos; I lived among upper class Catholic, conservative Mexicans and moved in circles of Mexican intellectuals of various political faiths.

3. In Mexico practically everybody is of mixed Caucasian-Mongoloid stock and the "Utopians" do not differ in their appearance (and range of skin shade) from other middle and upper-middle class Mexicans.

4. There are, indeed, several such native groups coming to Mexico City to dance—as I was able to see myself; none of them, however, is apparently associated with the Movement of Reappearance of Anauak, as I was assured by one of the Movement's members.

5. Data from a page attached to a book by María del Carmen Nieva, *Mexikayotl, (Esencía del Mexicano; Filosofía Nauatl)*, (Mexico City: Editorial Orion, 1969). This page is dated 1970.

6. *Op. cit.*, 1957, 1959, 1964.

7. *Op. cit.*, 1964.

8. *Op. cit.*, 1969.

9. Rodolfo Nieva left an unpublished manuscript of Nahua philosophy, which was edited and enlarged after his death by his sister and collaborator María del Carmen Nieva Lopez, *op. cit.*, 1969.

10. It is customary during anthropological congresses in Mexico to make short speeches in Nahuatl, and occasionally such Nahuatl speeches are made during other public gatherings as well.

11. Maria del Carmen Nieva Lopez, *Izkalotl Texto: Nauatl—Español—Ingles* (Mexico Tenochtitlan, 1972). The term "Mexican" and the language's name

"Mexica" is used interchangeably with "Nahuas" (people) and "Nahuatl" (language), p. 13.

12. In presenting this history I am relying mainly on the articles from *Izkalotl* rather than on scholarly writings of the Movement's historians, some of which I read, and some of which I was not able to locate.

13. Greeks are here, obviously, confused with Romans.

14. Main roads in Anauak were, apparently, "paved with stones, and were superior to European roads from this period." (*Izkalotl*, June 1962).

15. Comprising "North Americans," that is, mainly U.S. nationals.

16. Aleksander Hertz, *Szkice o Ideologjach* (Paryz: Instytut Literaeki, 1961).

17. Nieva Lopez, *op. cit.*, 1969, pp. 129-30.

18. I am grateful to Iris Andreski for her help with putting this appeal into the antiquated English.

19. Juan Luna Cárdenas, "Antecedentes Aztekah del Primer Congreso de Anauak" in *Memoria del Symposium Nacional de Historia Sobre el Primer Congreso Anauak* (Mexico City: Sociedad Mexicana de Geografía y Estadística, 1964).

20. Nieva Lopez, *op. cit.*, 1969.

21. The coming great cataclysm is sometimes presented as a result of nuclear warfare; sometimes as a collapse of occidental civilization; sometimes as a geological catastrophe prophesied "for the era of Aquarius" or as ecological collapse (exhaustion and pollution of resources).

22. This term is used for description of the St. Simonists by Lewis Coser, *Men of Ideas* (New York: Free Press, 1965), Chapter 9.

23. Called also *Calmécac* in anthropological literature.

24. Usually spelled Cuitláhuac in anthropological literature.

25. Extended family or clan-based communities with communal land and corporate social structure. A good analysis of precolonial *calpullis* is presented in Jacque Soustelle's *La Vie Cotidienne des Azteques* (*op. cit.*), p. 32. The Movement's members call them *"Kalpullis."*

26. For a good description of Mexican *ejidos* (agrarian communities) see Nathan L. Whetten, *Rural Mexico* (Chicago: The University of Chicago Press, 1948).

27. Ignacio Romerovargas, *Organización Política de los Pueblos de Anauak* (Published by the author, Mexico City, 1957).

28. A collection of exceptionally unfair and aggressive polemics with controversial but sober articles by Eulalia Guzman may be found in a collection of articles (published in Mexican Press) by Alfonso Trueba, *Doña Eulalia, Mestizo, y Otros Temas* (Mexico City: Editorial Jus, 1959).

29. The names of the elected officials and Movement's members are omitted in this context. Exaggerated discretion is better than unnecessary publicity.

30. I am acquainted with two books by the same author: María del Carmen Nieva, *Mexicayotl—Esencia del Mexicano, op. cit.*, and María del Carmen Nieva Lopez, *Izkalotl (Texto: Nauatl—Español—Ingles)* (Mexico Tenochtitlan, 1972).

31. As, for instance, a book by Virgilio Valladeres Aldeco, *El Verdadero Americano*, as noted in *Izkalotl* of September 1967.

32. *Izkalotl* of May 1972 states that the following authors:

"Jacque Soustelle; German Scholar Koeller; Swiss writers, Rafael Girard and Gertrude Duby; and Ruíz Martinez, *España Desnuda* (Madrid, 1916);

"Ignacio Romerovargas, Organización Política de los Pueblos de Anauak (Published by the author, Mexico, 1957);

"Ignacio Romerovargas, *Montezuma el Magnífico y la Invasión de Anauak*, Seleccíon de Estudios de la Sociedad Mexicana de Geografía y Estadística, Mexico, 1964;

"Ignacio Romerovargas, "Las Instituciones de Anauak" in *Esplendor de México Antiguo*, (Mexico City: Centro de Investigaciones Antropologicas de México, 1959);

"Juan Luna Cárdenas, "Antecedentes Aztekah del Primer Congreso de Anauak," in *Memoria de Symposium Nacional de Historia Sobre el Primer Congreso de Anauak*, (Mexico City: Sociedad Mexicana de Geografía y Estadística, 1964;

"Eulalia Guzman, *Relaciones de Hernán Cortés*;

"Ibarra Fortino de Anda, *Mexico Acreedor en la Civilización Mundial* as cited in *Izkalotl*, October 1967"—have been highly approved by the Movement.

33. According to "Ingeniero X," three to four thousand issues of the monthly magazine *Izkalotl* are generally published and the transformation of this monthly into a daily was not planned for 1973.

34. *Op. cit.*, 1966, p. 30.

35. Some Nahuas have been acculturated centuries ago to various other native groups and this process has continued. This type of complex qualitative differentiation cannot be shown in this simple diagram.

36. I read in *Izkalotl* about some PTA's and some college clubs being transformed into *calpullis* as well!

37. Nieva Lopez, *op. cit.*, 1969.

38. *Ibid.*

39. Nieva Lopez, *op. cit.*, 1969.

40. Licenciado Rodolfo Nieva in Nieva Lopez, *op. cit.*, 1969, p. 19.

41. Erik Erikson, "Identity and Uprootedness in Our Times" in Hendrick M. Ruitenbeck (ed.), *Varieties of Modern Social Theory* (New York: E. P. Dutton & Co., Inc. 1963).

42. In Nieva Lopez, *op. cit.*, 1969, pp. 182-3.

43. In Nieva Lopez, *op. cit.*, 1969, pp. 221-4.

44. *Ibid.*

CONCLUSIONS

1. Staab, *op. cit.* I prefer the term "Indianism" to Staab's "Indigenism."

2. *Ibid.*

3. *Ibid.*

4. *Ibid.*

5. Alfonso Caso, *Indigenismo*, (Mexico City: Instituto Nacional Indigenista, 1958), p. 70.

6. Their position is formulated in a book by Arturo Warman, Margarita Nolasco Arma, Guillermo Bonfil, Mercedes Olivera de Vazquez, Enrique Valencia, *De eso que llaman antropología Mexicana* (Mexico City: Ed. Nuestro Tiempo, 1970); interesting polemics with some points made in this book (mainly attacks on the INI) can be found in Fernando Benitez, *Los Indios de Mexico: Tierra Incognita* (Mexico City: Ed. Era, 1972).

7. Juan Vicente Palerm Viquiera, "La presencia del problema Indigena" *Comunidad*, No. 42, April, 1973.

8. It should be remembered at this point that in the middle of the nineteenth century, Yaqui leader Juan Banderas was advocating the establishment of an Indian Nation (see Edward Spicer, *Cycles of Conquest* (Tucson, Arizona: University of Arizona, 1962) p. 338), a fact which, probably, impressed the historically minded intellectuals from the Movement of Reappearance of Anauak, far more than Yaqui's "racial purity."

9. Emil Durkheim, *Division of Labour in Society* (New York: Free Press, 1964).

10. The relationship between ideology and outlook on life of the average man is discussed throughout Eric Fromm's writings.

11. A very sophisticated study of *Social Character in a Mexican Village* can be found in a book under this title by Eric Fromm and Michael Macoby, Prentice Hall, New York, 1970.

12. Such as military dictatorship or bloody semipermanent civil war, characteristic of Latin America in recent years.

13. I have in mind mainly such countries as Germany and Italy before the Second World War and those countries which were under their influence.

14. There were few dangerous incidents of such suppressions of freedom in contemporary Mexico, however, they always provoked strong protests.

15. Miguel S. Wionczek y otros autores, *Crecimiento o Desarollo Economico*, (Mexico City: SepSetentas, 1971).

16. Coser, *op. cit.*

17. *Ibid.*